Dear fear,

20 Powerful Lessons On Living Your Best Life
On The Other Side Of Fear

Tiana Patrice
Visionary Author

Tiana Patrice
info@tianapatrice.com

Ordering Information:
Quantity sales: Special discounts are available on quantity purchases by corporations, associations, and others. For details, contact the publisher at the address above.

Published by KLC Publishing
Printed in the United States of America
Designed By P2P Branded – www.p2pbranded.com

This book is intended to push you from the place that fear is attempting to keep you bound. This book is not intended to provide financial, health or legal advice. Please seek the appropriate counsel for financial, health or legal matters.

"Our deepest fear is not that we are inadequate. Our deepest fear is that we are powerful beyond measure. It is our light, not our darkness that most frightens us. We ask ourselves. Who am I to be brilliant, gorgeous, talented, and fabulous? Actually, who are you not to be? You are a child of God."

~Marianne Williamson~

To every woman who has allowed fear to punk her
out of her purpose...
this book is dedicated to you.

Table Of Contents

1. Intro
2. How To Use This Book
3. Dear Fear, You Can't Have My New Thing
4. Dear Fear, You Can't Have My Future
5. Dear Fear, You Can't Have My Mind
6. Dear Fear, You Can't Have My Life
7. Dear Fear, You Can't Have My Confidence
8. Dear Fear, You Can't Have My S.H.I.N.E.
9. Dear Fear, I Am Not Her
10. Dear Fear, You Can Keep Your Traditions
11. Dear Fear, You Can't Take My Breaking
12. Dear Fear, You Can't Have My Story
13. Dear Fear, You Can't Have My Dream
14. Dear Fear, You Can't Have My Greatness
15. Dear Fear, You Can't Have My Transition
16. Dear Fear, You Can't Have My Journey
17. Dear Fear, You Can't Have My Voice
18. Dear Fear, You Can't Have My Faith or Authenticity
19. Dear Fear, Let Go Of My Bootstraps
20. Dear Fear, You Can't Have My Position
21. Dear Fear, You Can't Have My Past
22. Dear Fear, You Can't Have My Impact

Intro

Fear is a consistent hustler. It hustles us to believe that we are inadequate to do the very thing God created us to do. It comes in like a thief in the night, lurking around our hopes, and our aspirations, to steal our light and leave us sitting in a dark room of broken and unachieved dreams. Fear is a consistent hustler. Never stopping, because it has a job to do, and that is to keep us from our greatness. Now, if fear is that consistent, shouldn't we be more consistent in our faith, our affirmations, our praise and our actions? The answer is yes! But why is it so hard to do? After all, the same energy it takes to give our fears power, is the very same energy it takes to give our faith power. In those moments that we choose fear over faith, we tell God that we don't trust him and instantly belittle our royalhood. So yes, I decided to dedicate this book to every single woman that has allowed fear to punk her out of her purpose. Why? Well for one you deserve it! For far too long fear has convinced us that we didn't matter, that our stories weren't worth telling, and our dreams weren't worth mentioning. Fear, while a taboo topic, is the most necessary conversation to have. Why? Because fear is the very reason why we aren't moving forward in our careers, and why we aren't launching our businesses. Fear is the reason we have become comfortable with mediocrity and look at success as something saved for the 1%. But the truth of the matter is, you are afraid to even admit you are afraid. The irony.

Fear has convinced you that in admitting you are afraid you are weak and vulnerable. Admitting you are afraid must mean that your cape has holes in it. In turn you continue doing life the same way, getting the same results and pretending like you are happy with it. But what if...in this moment you admitted that the reason you haven't truly operated in your purpose is because of fear. And the reason you haven't answered God's calling for your life is because of fear. Do you know how much power there is in acknowledging your truth? When you acknowledge that you are afraid you can then take action against fear, and create a plan that will allow you to do the very thing fear is convincing you that you can't do. Can I be honest with you? I almost didn't write this book because of fear. You and I now have something in common, we are connected by our common denominator. We can begin to take action, together, against that one thing holding us back. Fear. Do you know how powerful we become? How unstoppable we can be? That's exactly why I am on a mission to share stories of women all over the world. That's why I created the movement A Million Fearless Strong, because together we are fearless and strong.

In this book you will find 20 stories from powerful women with different backgrounds, but share that common denominator. Understand that it takes serious courage to tell these stories. It takes operating and activating your fearless to pull skeletons out of the closet, or come out of hiding. However these women did just that. Why? Because their stories give you an opportunity to say "me too" and to know that you aren't alone. Their stories give you hope. Their stories teach resilience. Their stories give you the strategies you need to live your best life on the other side of fear. Did you know that there is a life waiting for you, on the other side of your fear? You deserve to experience the greatness waiting for you. You deserve to experience life, fully charged and purposed. You. Deserve. I'm so excited for what happens next as you take this journey to the other side of your fear.

With Hugs & Love,
Tiana Patrice

How To Use This Book:

This book is meant to be more than just read. It is meant to transform your way of thinking, inspire you to dream bigger than you've ever dreamt, and give you the tools to take immediate action against your fear. In order to take immediate action against your fear, you must first acknowledge what you are afraid of.

Some common fears that I have come to know through my movement #AMillionFearlessStrong, are:

Fear of rejection
Fear of complacency
Fear of divorce
Fear of failure
Fear of success
Fear of the past
Fear of mediocrity

And the list goes on and on...what about you? Take some time to acknowledge your fear

I have a fear of _____
    But on this day of _____**, I am**
    making the bold and courageous choice to take action
    against my fears, and live the life destined for me.

Signed,

_____

Aren't you ready to take action? Aren't you ready to stop allowing fear to keep you playing small and breathing in the air of mediocrity? You are bold. You are royal. You are deserving. You are excellent. And fear, has no more power over your life.

Now, it's time for you to get in on this "Dear Fear" action! Take some time and write your own letter to fear:

Dear Fear,

_____

_____

_____

_____

_____

_____

_____

_____

_____

_____

_____

_____

_____

_____

_____

_____

_____

_____

_____

_____

_____

                              Signed,

Step 2: Take a quick photo of your letter against fear, and head over to social media. Post your photo and tag @tianapatrice using #DearFearBook #ActivateYourFearless #AMillionFearlessStrong

Step 3: Join the movement over at www.amillionfearlesstrong.org and invite 5 of your friends to join with you. Together we are A Million Fearless Strong.

We are on a mission to liberate women from the fear that's holding them back in life, career and business. So join the movement!

dear fear, you can't have my ...

NEW THING

BY TIANA PATRICE

Dear fear,

You Can't Have My New Thing

◆————————————————————————◆

It's officially been 2 years since my best-selling book *Fifty Two Shades Of Fearless* hit the shelves. I remember it like it was yesterday, so afraid to step into the thing God was calling me to do. So afraid to become everything God was calling me to become. And like many of you, so afraid to acknowledge that I, the girl who was so strong, was also so afraid. Why? Because I didn't know all of the answers. I was afraid because the vision seemed so far out of my reach. What would life look like when I decided to make the leap into unknown territory? Who would be there to help and support me? What if I failed? What if I succeeded, and now all eyes were on me? Those were the many questions that kept me up at night. How many of you can relate with these thoughts?

I wrote Fifty Two Shades Of Fearless in the saddest season of my life. I had just lost my grandmother and life seemed pretty dreadful. How many of you were raised by a single mom and a praying grandmother? That was me. And here I was being forced to live without the very one that taught me how too. The irony. In this season, I lost my desire to work with anyone. My business was fueled by my gifts and creativity, and it's hard to be creative when you're sad. In this season, I asked God to show me his will because I didn't know my purpose anymore. In that moment, God told me that my purpose was still the same, but my position in life was getting ready to change. I need somebody, right now, to catch that. Do you know that your position in life is getting ready to change? And as always, God was right. He ushered me right into my Isaiah 43:19 season.

See, I am doing a new thing! Now it springs up; do you not perceive it? I am making a way in the wilderness and streams in the wasteland.

God said I am getting ready to bring forth new things, do you not see that thing? Can you not perceive it? Understand that new things may be scary, but they are necessary for your growth. New things are God's promise to you. God said you may have never seen it done before, but I'm bringing it forth for you. He said that he is making a way in the wilderness and streams in the wasteland. Understand that your wilderness may look different from mine. But aren't you ready for your new thing?

God wanted me to write a book that would transform the lives of women all over the world. My assignment was to use my story to reach back and pull forward his purpose driven women and liberate them from the fear holding them back. And while I was afraid...I wrote. And when I didn't know all of the answers...I researched. And when I was tired...I brewed some tea and wrote some more. Even though at the time, I was grieving and my finances were dwindling. I wrote, I prayed and I wrote some more. And in 2 months, I had created the very thing Fear had convinced me that I couldn't. A best-selling book.

You see, fear was trying to keep me from my new thing. Fear had done its best to steal my voice and convince me that my story didn't matter. It crept in and attempted to kill my dreams by telling me my dreams were too big for a kid raised on the west side of Dothan, Alabama to reach. It pushed me in a dark room and tried to destroy my hopes and make me believe that I would never be on stages with greats and share my message with the world. What I grew to realize was that fear was no more than the enemy. And the enemy's plan is always to steal, kill and destroy the people that God has called forth. But I learned that while fear was big, my God is so much bigger.

What has God called you to do, that you have been so afraid to do? My advice to you is do it, and do it now. If you're afraid, admit it, but do it anyways. Do it alone, if you have too. Do it, no matter what others may think. Do it. Every time you take a step afraid, God will give you the provision to match your vision. Every time you take a step without all of the answers, God will align your steps and provide the clarity you need. Every time you take a step without the support you wanted, God will put you in position to get the support you needed. He has a new set of people waiting just for you! Don't allow fear to delay your destiny. Your new thing is waiting.

About the Author

Tiana Patrice is an award-winning global speaker, executive coach and best-selling author of the book Fifty Two Shades Of Fearless: Powerful Declarations For The Purpose Driven Woman and the visionary author for the highly anticipated book, Dear Fear. She is the owner of her global company, Women's CEO Alliance, a full service consulting company where she conducts workshops for companies and organizations on being a Fearless Leader in life, career and business, and provides intentional business, branding and marketing strategies to executive leaders, corporations and business owners. Tiana is also a member of the Forbes.Com Coaches Council, where she partners with

Forbes to share her message of living bold and fearless. She is a highly sought after speaker for industry and professional groups like Women's Economic Forum, Hyundai, and Peak Performers Institute, where she shared her message globally with more than 30,000 leaders. Other organizations for which she has shared her success tactics and expertise include: The Small Business Administration, Delta Sigma Theta, Dothan Area Chamber of Commerce, Troy State University, and many others. She is indeed the one to call if you are tired of letting fear hold you back in life, career and in business. Hailed as The Fearless Activator by her peers, Tiana helps her audience realize their fullest potential, let go of self-limiting beliefs, divorce their comfort zone and take immediate action on the other side of fear. For speaking inquiries, email info@tianapatrice.com. For more information on Women's CEO Alliance, head to www.womensceoalliance.com.

FUTURE

BY KHLOE LEE

dear fear, you can't have my ...

Dear fear,

You Can't Have My Future

◆————————————————————◆

My name is Khloe, and I'm 6 years old. My mom is the visionary author of this book. I know you may be thinking, wow she's so young, what can she teach me about fear. Well, just keep reading. You'll be surprised what you can learn from my adventures. I remember the day my mom announced she was writing a book with other authors. I was so excited for her, and immediately saw this as my chance to get in one of mommy's books.

Me: Mom, why can't I be an author in your book?
Mom: Well Khloe, tell me. If you were an author in the book, what would you talk about?
Me: I could talk about how I was afraid to ride my bike, but how I did it anyway.
Mom: That's a great story, with powerful lessons. I would love to have you in the book. And what would you call your chapter?
Me: Dear Fear, You Can't Have My Future.

Here's the thing, it's not often you get a lesson on fear from a 6 year old. If I may be honest, it's not often I am afraid of anything. I think bugs are pretty cool and I will try any flip, twist or turn (future Gabby Douglas in the making) with the best of them. But the reality is, even I have had experiences with fear. However, being raised by the Fearless Activator, Tiana Patrice, does not leave much room for allowing fear to win.

I remember the day mommy told me it was time to learn to ride my bike. I was so afraid. The night before, I laid in bed fearful, anticipating the day ahead. Usually I am the first to rise in the morning, waking everyone in the house. But not this day. On this day, I took my time waking up and getting out of bed. I didn't run to wake mommy up like I normally do. To be honest, I was hoping that she had a short case of amnesia and forgot about teaching me to ride the knee scraper on wheels. Boy was I wrong. Within 2 minutes of mommy waking up, I heard those awful words. "Khloeeee, today you learn to ride your bike. Are you excited?" In my head I came up with 100 excuses not to learn, but the one that came out was, "Mommy, my dolly is sick. I can't learn today." Hey listen, it was the best I could come up with at that time. But of course, mommy wasn't hearing that. When that woman sets her mind to something there is no stopping her. Finally, we made our way outside, and the moment to put up or give up arrived. I'm staring at my bike. My bike was staring at me. And I was terrified. Fear was punking me, and I was absolutely ok with it. I bet you can relate, right? I imagined every possible thing that could go wrong. "Mommy, what if I fall," I said, hoping she would hear my plea. Instead she said, "Khloe, you just may fall, that's life. Just get back up and keep trying." It was then I realized two things. One, mommy is relentless, like seriously who is this woman? And two, I wasn't going to bed unless I rode this bike. Finally, I mustered up the courage to get on. And guess what!? I fell. I mean I fell like nobody's business. No kid should ever meet pavement for the first time in such a disrespectful way. I think for a moment the pavement felt bad for me. Like seriously, I think I heard it chuckle. But mommy just picked me up, dusted me off and put me back on the bike.

While she was getting me ready to try again, she showed me a scar on her knee where she fell as a kid. Wow! Mommy used to be a kid! Who knew? Hearing her story made me more comfortable, and I wanted to try again. This time I knew a different way to do it. After about 6 more times of meeting my new friend, pavement, I got it right. And I rode that bike like I was its boss. And you know what? I had a blast! Sure I was scraped up a little bit, but when I pushed through my fear, there was fun waiting for me on the other side. And now, I can teach another kid how to ride a bike and how to avoid the mistakes I made.

I may only be 6, but what I've learned is when you fall, get back up and keep trying because there is fun waiting for you on the other side. My future depended on me pushing through what made me uncomfortable, and now I can help someone else do the same. Just like mommy shared her story with me, I now have a story I can share with someone else! That's the great thing about falling. It doesn't mean failing, unless you choose not to get back up. And that's a choice only you can make because life is about choices. When you get up, you get up with a story. And you're stronger. And you're confident. And that makes you fearless.

In what areas of your life are you afraid to try because you are afraid to fall?

_____

_____

_____

What action can you take today, right now, to push beyond that fear and do it anyway?

_____

_____

_____

About the Author

Khloe Lee is a fearless gymnast, entrepreneur and author with a knack of turning everyday situations into laugh out loud experiences. Every day she takes her audience on a journey of laughter and love as she shares her experiences about life through her eyes. Learn more about Khloe and her upcoming book, Fearless Little Me at www.theadventuresofkhloelee.com.

Dear fear, you have no place here, you have no place in this space. I know that what God had for me is greater than the fear and anxiety you desire to produce in me, and I will always keep the people I am called to first, which means you will have to take a back seat.

Patrice Cunningham Washington
www.realmoneyanswers.com

dear fear, you can't have my...

MIND

BY JAY ANISE

Dear fear,

You Can't Have My Mind

•————————————————————————•

I, Jay Anise, was a sell out! Those words are ideal in the description of who I was for over 10 years of my life. Why? Because I allowed fear to control my mind and how I viewed myself. I sacrificed my endless possibilities for worldly acceptance. I betrayed my true self by abandoning my life's purpose in order to reside in a place filled with self-destructive thoughts. I discarded the positive and nurtured the negative. I built a home with my #1 enemy, FEAR!

Can you relate?

I remember going to the circus and having a true epiphany moment. While I was enjoying the tricks and acts, I realized that I was looking at a direct reflection of my life. You see, at one point it seemed that I was the person performing the acts, and I felt that the audience waited anxiously to see if I would succeed or fail. There was so much pressure to be immaculate with all eyes on me. What would "they" think if I stumbled? It was as if I stood on the tightrope, wondering who would be laughing when I messed up. I looked throughout the crowd and everyone was on the edge of their seats. I was hoping someone would stand and cheer me on, but no one did. I was filled with worry, doubt, and thoughts of my incapability of reaching the other side. I was unable to focus due to this mindset and as I took my first step, I slipped.

Have you ever tried to take a leap of faith in your life, but you were so concerned with what others would think that you found yourself defeated before you even started?

As the audience ridiculed me, I began to recognize many faces. Their hair, their skin, their smiles...they ALL resembled mine. "They", were me. The judgmental individual that I was so afraid to disappoint was ME! I didn't fail because others didn't believe in me. I failed because I did not believe in myself. I failed because I did not have faith in my ability to attain great outcomes. I failed because I could not even stand up for myself. I was a sellout. I sold out to fear!

"I'm so emotionally and mentally defeated by me. Non believer in self and my ability to succeed. Surrounded by what seems to be a pool of my own blood. Fully submerged in a sea of self-inflicted insecurity. I'm drowning."

~Jay Anise (The Comparison)

28

My lack of self-confidence commenced at a young age. It was not, however, due to the absence of positive role models. For every negative thought I had about myself, my parents stated a positive. For every tear that was shed, I had a cousin telling me that everything would be alright. Yet somehow, I still felt alone. In grade school I was teased for having big eyes, a deep voice, and a face painted with acne. My hair wasn't long, I wore glasses and braces at one point, and I didn't have any "meat on my bones" as some would say. I didn't feel beautiful. Like most young girls, I began to equate beauty with outward appearance only. I never once acknowledged the beauty inside of me. I began putting on makeup just to go to the ATM or to the gas station (even though I was paying at the pump). I despised looking at myself in the mirror. I had allowed others to plant such an ugly seed, and I watered that seed daily until it grew into a broken flower.

Broken, ugly and abused on the inside, I started to covet other people's blessings. I used social media as a platform to feed my negative mindset. My constant thoughts were, "I wish I was married. I can't believe I'm not in my career yet. She's doing so well, what's wrong with me?" Can you relate? Let me stop here to let you know this. There is absolutely NOTHING wrong with you! To whom are you comparing yourself? Answer that question (out loud). Now, STOP it! God made you special. You were made to follow your own path, which may not be an easy route. Your path may be to do something that has never been done before, and it may be difficult. But you don't have to be like anyone else to reach your dreams. And just because another is succeeding doesn't mean that you will fail.

There is one thing I can guarantee. You will fail 100% of the time trying to be someone that you're not. Congratulate someone today and learn to be proud of those doing great things, don't envy. You don't know their story and they don't know yours. The best gift you can offer the world is the gift of being YOU. You don't have to be like anyone else, you are wonderfully made and perfect just the way you are.

This is a lesson that I have finally come to realize, so I am on assignment to share it with you. However it took me failing, and dealing with rejection over and over again to get to this point. I had to learn that failing means I took action. And action is what leads to success.

"It's ok to fail. If I fail, at least I know I tried to do something.
If I don't try to do anything, nothing will ever happen."
~ Jay Anise ~

One of my hardest failures was when I failed my NCLEX exam to become a nurse. It was one of *the* lowest seasons of my life. How could this happen? I attended a *private* college and graduated Magna Cum Laude, in the top of my class. But I failed. I was embarrassed, defeated, and filled with negative energy. *As people all around me were passing, I began to devalue myself.* And while I was busy sulking, fear was waiting for its chance to re-enter my space. Fear convinced me that I wasn't good enough. Fear took me back to my childhood, and that ugly, broken girl *resurfaced.* Fear told me I would fail again, so why try? And so, I didn't. With a Bachelor's degree in Nursing, and with scores from the top of my class, I sold out to fear again. For one year, I unloaded trucks at Toys R Us, while my career that I surely deserved collected dust in the background.

Have you ever failed at something and are now afraid to try again? I'll tell you this, you deserve much more than settling for complacency. I had to learn that NO does not mean NEVER! Only you can claim that you've been defeated, and why would you accept that as your fate? Stop claiming defeat as your destiny!

After a year of settling for less than my best, I became ready for change. I still had negative thoughts, but this time I decided to turn to and seek help from God. I let him into my situation, prayed, and tithed continuously. I remembered that God gave us his only Son so that we wouldn't have to fight our battles alone. I scheduled a new time to take my exam, and while everything that could have gone wrong on that day did, I didn't allow that to steal my joy. And I passed! When I shifted my mind, my world changed. When I replaced my fear with faith, my life expanded. And within one month, I had my first nursing job and a brand new car! Won't he do it?

You see, fear has a job to do. And that is to stop you from achieving your greatness. I encourage you on this day, to take back your mind. Take back your thoughts and stand on your faith. Don't miss your blessings because you continue to sell out to fear. Is it going to be easy? No. Is it worth it? Yes. A little struggle and sacrifice will yield your success.

Over the next few years I continued to have constant fights with fear and faith. *I knew the power of positive thinking but I harbored the negative.* I could not release past pain long enough to appreciate present favor. However, faith always prevailed. That's why I am here to share my story. I became a mom, I lost my father, I lost myself. I wanted to give up. But faith, prevailed. During my weakest moment, I experienced a dynamic shift in my life while at my home church. I had people to go above and beyond to ensure my well being. This in turn, assisted in me fighting for my mind...fighting for my life! It began to sink in that my son deserved a Mommy that would reach her fullest potential. And I am doing just that!

Getting to this point was only the beginning. It still takes constant work to hold on to this new found mindset. Just like a relationship, we can't expect to work hard to get somewhere but not work hard to keep it! So are you ready to do the work? Are you tired of allowing fear to control your mind?

Here are a few things that I do to keep me grounded and moving forward.

1.

I maintain a strong relationship with God.

I acknowledge him as the head of my life, tithe, pray, and study my word. I listen to him when he speaks. I trust God's process and move when/where he leads.

2.

I ask for help.

A lot of times, we as women, feel that we must always be strong and have everything figured out. That can become overwhelming, right? It's true that everyone may not be for you, but that doesn't mean everyone is against you. Confide in a close friend, a loved one, or a mentor. You may be holding things in and they may have a solution. I pushed my "superwoman mentality" to the side and was able to release some much needed frustration and concerns. I got a life coach, and it was an amazing decision. I had a few sessions that opened my mind to the idea of me starting a business. I thought I wasn't capable, and he gave me exercises that helped prove to myself that I am. Then I began coaching with Tiana Patrice who helped me break down my walls of fear so I could execute ideas and move in my purpose. She was a true Godsend.

Who is 1 person that you can confide in today, to begin taking back the reigns of your life?

_____

When will you reach out to this person?

_____

3.
I faced my fears head on.

I am nervous when I go into a room to perform my spoken word, but I do it anyway. If I don't speak, someone may be missing a message that they need. My heart was racing at my first event but I pushed through my fear and delivered. By performing that night, other doors were opened.

What have you been afraid to do?

_____

What date will you get this done?

_____

4.

I stopped wearing my old shoes!

Let's say that your favorite pair of shoes are now worn out and too small. You love those shoes, and those are the ones you are most comfortable in. You can't fathom the idea of letting them go, but nothing positive is coming from keeping them. So instead of leveling up into the shoes you deserve, you keep wearing them. *And now you are experiencing constant pain and regret.* What in your life is too small and out of date?

Write at least 3 things that you need to release in order to move forward into the life you deserve.

    1. _____

    2. _____

    3. _____

5.

When I find negative thoughts brewing, I speak positive.

It sounds simple, but it can be challenging. It's like riding a bike. The more you do it, the more you'll get the hang of it. This is a tough one for me, but an absolute must! Try it! Instead of saying, "I'll always live paycheck to paycheck", say "I know my increase is coming." Instead of saying, "Things will never change", say, "I may not be able to see it but God is working on my behalf. Things are about to change." This made a HUGE difference in my life. List one negative thought you've been having and how you can speak it positively.

Negative Thought   Positive Talk

_____   _____

6.

I stopped dwelling in the past.

The only time you should look over your shoulder is when you are looking back to celebrate the obstacles you have overcome. Learn to be appreciative of what your struggles and hardships have helped you to become. Be proud of yourself. *If you are doing anything to work towards your dreams or better yourself, then that is progress*! Don't wait to reach the finish line to appreciate your growth. Each accomplishment matters, big or small. Be proud of who you are WHILE becoming who you know you can be. That will enhance your self motivation and nothing will be able to stop you!

7.

LESS = More

I LISTEN to motivational videos or songs that get me pumped up. I ENGAGE in inspirational discussions with my peers. I SPEAK positive affirmations over my life, most times while looking in a mirror (i.e. you are smart, you are beautiful, you can do anything that you put your mind to, etc.). *I read as well as write down things that I love about myself.* By doing this I can SEE on paper how great I am, just in case my mind tries to get in the way. Write down 3 things you love about yourself and add to it daily!

1. _____

2. _____

3. _____

"Listening, Engaging, Speaking, and Seeing yields More Freedom, More Success, and More Stability."

~ Jay Anise ~

"You have a choice to make. If you continue on this path you will be eradicated. But you can travel a different route and redirect your mind. So what will it be, the grave or life in your eyes? I hope loving me is what you deicide."

~ Jay Anise (What Will It Be)

At the end of it all, I chose me! *I put others first for a long time and I finally decided that I deserved putting myself first. I realized that my life doesn't work without me!* I fell in love with me, Jay Anise, down to my core! And the best part of it all is that I am genuinely happy with every step that I take. This broken, ugly and abused flower has now bloomed into a beautiful, strong, and confident rose. If I can make it to the other side of fear and reclaim control of my mind, so can you!

I believe in you! So say it with me, **"Dear Fear, You Can't Have My Mind!"**

About the Author

Jasmine "Jay Anise" Hendrix is a songwriter, spoken word artist, co-author, and mother to a handsome boy, Kalib. She is founder of Never Outta Ink LLC, which is a business started to inspire and motivate others through the power of words. Jay Anise is inspired by her mother Renee and 3 guardian angels, her father Walter, grandmother Mary, and stepfather Tyrone. Because she struggled with insecurities and lack of confidence in the past, and she hopes to empower anyone who is dealing with the same. Her personal mission is to touch lives and help transform minds! Learn more at www.neverouttaink.com and follow on all Social Media @jayanise

LIFE

BY STEPHANIE VALENTINE

dear fear, you can't have my ...my

Dear fear,

You Can't Have My Life

I remember my first feeling of fear as a little girl around 5 or 6 years old laying in the bed wide awake. My parents would be arguing in the middle of the night after my Dad would come in late from the bar. I would lie there fearful that my dad would then turn that rage onto me. It was then I learned to be quiet, my feelings didn't matter. I remember the fear of the first day of elementary school unlike others who were excited to see old friends, I was fearful that I wouldn't have any friends. I was the one who knew all the answers, and because of that I would be picked on by my peers. It was then I learned to not shine so bright just so I could fit in. I remember being afraid to be left home with my sister because she was so mean to me and would find any reason to hit me. When I told my mother, she said it was just "sibling rivalry" but it wasn't. I was too young to stand up for myself and it was then I learned to ignore abuse. I let fear teach me things that weren't true and allowed it to tell me how I should feel and act. Can you see how by the age of 10 fear was my best friend?

It's hard at times for an adult to deal with their fears, imagine being 10 years old, living in fear of just being yourself. Crazy, right? I could only be me when I was by myself, playing with my dolls and imagining a world where I was in control. I wasn't told to be quiet. I wasn't told to stop asking questions. I wasn't fearful of being me, having and doing whatever I wanted. As you can imagine, being pushed into a shell and afraid to be me, slowly turned into anger. "You're not smart enough, you act dumb, you're too quiet, that's not your personality." someone once told me. I wanted to scream out "how would you know, you don't even know me." On the outside I was the prim and proper child that my Mother had raised but inside the anger begin to fester within me and it had nowhere to go. I needed to process my feelings and the only way I knew how, was to write. Whatever came to mind, I wrote it. Someone made me mad? I wrote about it. Something terrible happened at school, I wrote about it. Something happen at home that I couldn't share with anyone, I wrote about. Sometimes I had no words I just drew shapes and lines. At an early age fear had taught me that the only way to live was just to accept what others had already pre-destined for me. What others had already said I would be was who I would become. My anger had come from fear silencing and stripping me of my voice. Before I learned to drive, fear had already driven away my dreams. I let fear take away my dream of leaving home and going away to college. I let fear tell me, I needed to be at home, I wasn't strong enough to be away from my family. I let fear tell me not to apply for jobs I knew I was qualified for but telling myself I wasn't good enough. I let fear of not being enough keep me from so many things as a young adult. I gave up so many dreams because fear said, "you're not bold enough, you don't have enough money, you are a coward." And so I believed it...

The only thing that I held onto was my ability to dream of a life where I was free to be me. Those were the only things that fear could not take away from me.

Fear crept into my adulthood and every decision I made was guided by my fear. I remember the day, I got fed up and tired of letting fear keep me bound. I was at a conference in Atlanta in February 2014 and I remember my travel partner and I were back in the room debriefing about what we learned and our take-aways after the day's events. We began to talk about things and before I knew it, I felt comfortable enough to remove my mask and share all my pain, my insecurities and the things that held me back. The next thing you know I was crying the ugly cry, you know the one where tears are flowing uncontrollably, you can't breathe literally because snot is flowing like a faucet...yeah, that ugly cry. I was releasing everything that kept me bound as she prayed over me. It was a defining moment in my life that I will never forget. That day, I ejected fear from the driver's seat of my life and took the wheel back. I was tired of allowing fear to keep me held hostage. Tired of fear telling me what I can and can't do. I was in fight mode. Fear had robbed me of jobs I was qualified for. Fear has robbed me of loving relationships because I didn't think I was worthy of love. And fear had robbed me of my own pursuit of happiness. Tired of being broken-hearted, tired of being passed by on all my wants and desires while watching others prosper, grow and move to their next level. I was tired!

I refused to let another day, another month, another year pass me by. I refused to be in the same place on that day the following year. I was better than who I had allowed myself to become, I was greater than who I had allowed myself to become. God did not give me a spirit of fear. God did not give me those thoughts I wrote in my journal, the dreams I had imagined and the visions I had for myself and kids to be fearful of them.

When I returned home, I officially launched my girl's empowerment program, Be Candy Coated in April 2014 so that I could share my story. I shared the lessons I had learned that were written in all my journals, to empower and uplift the same girls who also felt they didn't have a voice. I didn't let fear keep me from helping the kids I once dreamt about teaching. It didn't stop there, God gave me the vision to help women who had been those same little girls wearing masks afraid to be themselves. The Maximize Your Zone movement for women was founded in March 2015. Fear could not stop me from pursuing my purpose of helping others live the life they desired. You see I had learned that what I had been through in my life that caused fear to take the driver seat were lessons not for me, but it was for the purpose of helping others. Fear tried to keep me from my purpose! Fear tried to keep me from my destiny by whispering in my ear all those years, just like a no-good man keeping you under his spell. But just like a relationship that has gone bad, eventually you wake up and kick that man to the curb. You have the power to live your life FEARLESS.

Now don't get me wrong, fear is still present, fear will still creep up and sneak in when you least expect it. Fear disguises itself in things that you want, things that you desire and yes even in people.

FEAR is strong, but YOU are stronger.

YOU are able to overcome it.

YOU have what it takes to do whatever YOU

put your mind to.

Once you step into the fear, once you face it head on...your FAITH automatically takes over. Fear has no chance to grow nor prosper. No weapon shall prosper when you walk in FAITH not Fear.

There are three things that I do to break through my fear, I would empower you to adopt into your mindset as well.

1) Acknowledge your fear – experience it and recognize it as JUST a feeling.

2) Be aware of HOW your fear is showing up – is it procrastination, is it overwhelm, is it avoidance?

_____

3) Describe the worst-case scenario that fear is leading you to believe? Has it happened before? What lessons were learned that you can use to move forward?

_____

_____

_____

Whenever you begin to start hearing that small voice saying you can't, you're not good enough, you're not smart enough, it won't ever work, I need you to say: Dear Fear, my life, you can NOT have.

About the Author

As an entrepreneur, business owner and mentor, Stephanie Valentine has built a reputation in the community as a strong supporter of women owned businesses and organizations in support of empowering and raising self- awareness within girls and women. Stephanie is no stranger to the area of personal development and seeking the greatness that dwells within. As an entrepreneur and business owner since 2009, Stephanie has worked to align her beliefs of self-awareness, serving and lifting as your climb, into her endeavors. In 2014, she created and launched Be Candy Coated, her own organization for girls' empowerment and wrote a curriculum that was successfully implemented to help them be confident and accepting of themselves. In 2015, she created the Maximize Your Zone movement for women, an online community where she offers tools, resources and support to women who are ready to confidently step into their next level. As a certified coach, business consultant and social media strategist, Stephanie assists entrepreneurs and small businesses in effectively increasing their visibility and credibility in the online arena, leading to growth and profitability. Learn more about Stephanie at www.maximizeyourzone.com

dear fear, you can't have my...

CONFIDENCE

BY MAKEITHIA DANIELS

Dear fear,

You Can't Have My Confidence

◆————————————————————————————————————◆

    If you're anything like me, you are very familiar with living in a "comfort zone". You know, that land where you play it safe, and nothing can harm you or hurt you there. My comfort zone was my place of refuge, it was my place of confinement...it was my prison. I find it ironic that we call it a comfort zone, because if we must be honest, are we really comfortable there? I'll let you take a moment to think about that! It was only when I began my journey to being confident that I realized, I didn't stay in my comfort zone out of comfort. I stayed because of fear.

    For each of us our comfort zone may look different. For me it consisted of going to work, home, church, and school, when I was enrolled. I allowed fear to convince me to be alone because of my introverted characteristics. Because I know that I am an introvert, it made agreeing with fear very easy. However, when I pulled back the layers, the truth was, I was afraid. I was afraid of being picked on and judged by others. This caused me to keep myself in seclusion so I wouldn't have to suffer the name calling that I was accustomed to when I was a little girl. I didn't want to relive the moments of getting off the bus and having older kids call me names. Can you relate at all? I learned early on that sticks and stones may break my bones, but also that words DO hurt! Words are sharp and painful. And no matter how much I sang that song in my head, it never stopped the pain.

On my journey to being confident, I learned to make the bold and conscious choice to step out of my comfort zone daily. On the days that I didn't want to, God purposely placed people in my life that pushed me into my purpose. I remember being in bed one Saturday morning about 7:30 AM, and of course I hopped on social media. I saw a notification that one of my sisters was going to an event near me. Ironically, it was Tiana Patrice's Fearless Photo shoot, promoting The Fearless Tour that was coming up. On this day, I made the decision to do something different, something outside of myself and attend the photo shoot. Initially the decision was easy because my sister was going to be there as well and it was FREE, and if you're like me you love FREE! Now don't get me wrong, I was no stranger to the camera. My phone holds an arsenal of selfies you wouldn't dare want to compete with me on (they don't call me the selfie queen for nothing). After checking out the details and confirming it wasn't too late for me to take part, I was on my way to my first professional photo shoot.

The attire was a white shirt and denim jeans. After I realized my white shirt had a stain on it, I went to Wal-Mart and got a white t-shirt and some fresh white Wal-Mart brand KED-like tennis shoes. I put a little makeup on (just eye makeup and some lip gloss) and I felt real cute and confident. In my Queen Bee voice, *I was feeling myself.* I thought I was going to be a little late, but I got there right on time. Little did I know, I had an unwanted visitor enter the room and took a seat right next to me...it was fear. As I sat and began to look around the room at the other women in attendance, I began to feel out of place. Hello fear. Bye, bye confidence.

For a brief moment I entertained fear in a conversation about my being there. I began to compare myself to the other women who seemed to be actual supermodels. Fear convinced me that I didn't belong because the women were prettier than I was, they were dressed better than I was, and they were smaller than I was. In that moment, without my permission, fear took me back to that little girl getting off the bus. Except this time, there were no bigger kids picking on me, it was just me picking on myself. I wanted to run. The Holy Spirit told me to wait. So I did. I stayed and I snapped myself back into reality. And the reality was, no I didn't look like the other women, but I had just as much right to be there. Hello confidence, I am so glad you're back!

It was on that day that I began to activate my fearLESS and no longer allow the fear of the opinions of others to keep me in confinement or what I was referring to as my "comfort zone." It was at that moment that I chose to evict myself from "the land of the they's." This is a place where I was always worried about what "they" say about me or what "they" think about me. In this land, the choices I made about my life were centered around the thoughts and opinions of the "they's." I had just finished having my knockout with fear and evicted myself from "the land of the they's," and I was back to feeling myself, but it didn't take fear long to creep back in. You see that's the thing about fear, fear is quite the lurker, always waiting for a moment to catch us slipping to doubt. And my moment was back again. All of the ladies were preparing to take group photos, and it seemed as if they had known one another for years. My sister, who was supposed to be there, never made it, so I didn't have a familiar face to pose with. I saw that as my moment to exit stage left, but Tiana would not allow me to play small. She strongly and lovingly suggested I just take pictures with some of the other ladies. I did, and the results were amazing.

The day of that photo shoot changed my life, ultimately because it changed how I see myself. I realized that true confidence comes from continuing to show up true to who you are, as you are, even when your confidence is challenged. On that day, I made the declaration that fear could not have my confidence. Since making the decision to do something different even if it scared me, my blessings have exceeded me. Can you celebrate with me for one minute?

1. I have boldly stepped into my purpose.
2. I launched the WeSlay Movement (Join myself and the amazing Slaysters by following us on Facebook!)
3. I got a coach! Yes, you guessed it. Tiana Patrice, or Coach T as we call her has supported me and guided me into new doors and opportunities I would have never imagined.
4. I learned to get out and live my best life by connecting with others, and not being intimidated by their greatness because I became confident in my own.
5. I have taken on stages as a bold and confident speaker!
6. I'm an author yall! Look, you're reading one of my books! Look at God!

What can stepping outside of your comfort zone do for you? I have this saying I share with my Slaysters about what confidence means to me that I want to share with you.

Confidence is, loving who you are, where you are, while reaching for the person you are purposed to be.

This means, that in order to reach the woman that we are destined to be, we must first accept and love the woman we are right now and learn from where we are. There are lessons I am learning every day that will help me successfully walk in my purpose. My new found confidence allows me to have the right mindset and attitude to learn those lessons and not be discouraged through the process. This journey is a daily task. Everyday opposition will arise and fear will turn it's swift tongue to your ears of insecurity, but you must remain strong, bold, and confident, and command fear to get on the couch, grab some popcorn and enjoy the show as you confidently and fearlessly walk in your purpose. Now let's celebrate you!

How has fear kept you playing small inside of your comfort zone?

_____

_____

_____

What are 3 ways you can begin to step out of your comfort zone today?

_____

_____

About the Author

Makeithia Daniels is an inspiring motivational speaker, aspiring full-figured model, and author! As founder of the WeSLAY Movement, Makeithia uses her growing platform to encourage, inspire, and motivate women and teens to love/accept who they are, where they are, while striving to be the person they are purposed to be. She is also the creator of the Facebook group Slaysters where she uses her voice to accomplish her mission and walk in her purpose of spreading and sharing the importance of being confident in who you are.

Dear fear, If you don't get out of my face and get your life we're going to have a serious problem, ok! I know you are there but you will not have any control over my thoughts, over my ideas, over the people I connect with or any growth of where I am going. I know you are there but you can ride on the sideline because you will not take first place in the development and growth of my life.

Audria Richmond
www.audriarichmond.com

SHINE

BY JASMINE DYSON

dear fear, you can't have my ...

You Can't Have My S.H.I.N.E
(My Success, my Happiness, my Influence, my Name,
or my Excellence)

"Who you allow in your ear will eventually buy your time
and purchase your destiny."
-Author Unknown

"You think you cute…, you not the only one who can…,
they didn't stop making -blank- when they made yours," were
all things I heard from family growing up. Whether it was the
clothes I wore, a new hairstyle or my report card, it seemed
like every day I was constantly apologizing for being proud of
the things I had or had accomplished. I can remember arguing,
fussing and fighting with my cousins daily about something I
said or did, that suggested I "thought I was better than them."
Because of this constant battle, I found myself trying to
apologize for my achievements, or hide them in fear of
someone feeling inferior. I began living my life always
apologizing for simply being….me.

Shine like the world is yours!

Growing up I was what you would consider the "poster child." The honor roll student, the dancer/athlete, the "cool kid" that was also respectful, and a leader not a follower. People were drawn to me, both adults and children - for what my old boss would call my "good energy." And while I appreciated the kind gestures, I didn't feel better than or less than because of it. You see, I was never on a mission to compete or out-do anyone else, I was just simply operating in my gifts. My mom had always told me that I was exceptional and that I could do ANYTHING – and who was I not to believe her? LOL. It's funny now, because as an adult I recently had a conversation with friends about goals, dreams and purpose. The revelation I gave to them was this –

"Most people don't succeed in achieving their goals and dreams because they don't believe enough to take ACTION."

So then the question becomes, what stops us from believing and then taking massive action? **FEAR!**

For me, fear is one of those ideals that I never really acknowledged. And if you're anything like me, you likely don't recognize it when it comes your way either. It creeps up on you like a thief in the night and convinces you that it's not what it appears to be. It distracts you into believing that your submission to fear is simply using "good judgement."

When I was younger and I began to shrink myself to appease others, I didn't see it as "fear." I saw it as respect or being what we would call "humble" *cues Kendrick Lamar verse*. Not until I grew older and more mature did I realize that I was truly operating out of fear. I wasn't afraid of the task itself, but the responsibility of holding the mantel. You see, people are drawn to light, so when you shine you agree to constantly have all eyes on you – something I grew to both love and hate. Was it not acceptable for me to fail or be just good enough (average)? That was the question I constantly asked myself.

For the first 10 years of my life, I was raised by a single mom. Although my Dad was a great provider, I didn't get to see or spend much time with him much. My mom comes from a small family, so it was pretty much just she, my uncle, grandmother and me. She kept me very busy, whether it was dance class, cheerleading practice, museums, the movies or the mall. I was always on the go, but as an only child I liked it that way. For as long as I can remember my mom had two rules – get good grades in school and be respectful of yourself and others. She always told me that I was exceptional and never allowed me to settle for second best. But sometimes I felt like I was being punished for doing just that. In middle school, I can remember being put out of class for being "uninterested and not paying attention." My science teacher could not stand me. She was so annoyed by the fact that I would finish an assignment in 10 minutes with 30-45 minutes left in class. For the rest of the time I would sit there and write, sleep or find some other way to entertain myself. I was not disruptive, loud or the class clown, I was simply not being challenged enough to be engaged the whole time. After writing me up and sending me to the principal's office for a parent/teacher conference, it was determined that I needed more to stay engaged, which meant "busy work" ***rolls eyes***. Everywhere I turned I was "offending" someone for not being average. As a child, that sounded like punishment to me. But what could I do to change something that I wasn't trying very hard at in the first place?

The Great Expectation...

You ever feel like you're standing in the middle of the room naked and everyone is staring at you? That's how I felt every day of my life. People expected me to be right, expected me to be strong and expected me to win. It was just TOO MUCH PRESSURE. Can you relate? As I got older, I started to rebel. I no longer wanted to be the girl who got it all right. I wanted to push the envelope, explore new things and just HAVE FUN. I was tired of the structure, the discipline, the rules and the expectations. I wanted to be carefree and regular (for me that meant mediocre). In school, my grades started to slip and I no longer wanted to do organized sports – my life was about socializing, parties and FUN.

In middle school, I hung with a group of girls and we called ourselves the "2Flyy Honeys." We were the popular girls in school, everybody liked us and they all wanted to hang with our crew. In DC, we have this music called "GoGo" and there are weekly shows where bands play live music at teen clubs. Apart of the GoGo culture are neighborhood crews or what people would consider "gangs" that frequented these events. Because we were popular and attended these events often, people associated our group with that same culture and challenged us often. I'll never forget, about a week before my 8th grade graduation, my friends and I got into this huge group fight after school – our crew against another group of girls who attended our school. Almost every one of my friends who participated immediately got expelled from school. In that moment, I remember being so disappointed in myself. Here I was, the straight A student who had just been accepted into the top high school in Washington, DC with a 100% college acceptance rate, facing expulsion for a "gang fight" at school a week before 8th grade graduation. I was sacrificing my future all because I didn't want to own my power and challenge myself and others to be better than average. Fear had convinced me that extraordinary was a threat, so I believed mediocrity was my salvation.

Don't let someone dim your light simply because it's shining in their eyes...

I was never the girl who needed to compete for attention. I was an only child with two wonderful parents who adored me, and quite frankly I was never really enthused by outside acceptance. For me, I always knew I was different. Not better, but different, and I owned that at a very young age.

When I first got to high school, I had one focus, COLLEGE. It was one of those non-negotiables for me in my household. No one in my family had a college degree, so that was to be the first of many generational curses that I was tasked to break. After partying and living it up in middle school, and almost giving this great opportunity away, it was time to get focused and excel. When I first stepped foot on that campus, it represented one thing for me, EXCELLENCE. It was a new environment where people didn't care much about anything except academics. It wasn't about who had on what, or when the next party would be (because there weren't any lol). We all had one common goal - to secure our future.

Talk about a humbling experience! I could no longer get by, by doing the _"bare minimum."_ I had to study, I had to do homework and I had to pay attention in class - ***rolls eyes***.

Looking back, it was just the challenge I needed to get back the SHINE that I allowed fear to take from me. You see, I'm one of those people who can just pick up on anything and teach it to myself. I'm an avid researcher and analytical thinker, so there's not much I can't figure out on my own. But boy when I tell you this was different *side eye*. I was asked to read/study Shakespeare, and learn statistics taught by a teacher who knew English as a second language, which had me completely in over my head. That coupled with the fact that we had no social activities and the school itself operated like a federal prison, I was NOT a happy camper.

Being at Banneker taught me a lot about perspective and the gift/curse of your environment. It's easy to shine or stand out in a room full of failure or darkness. But what do you do in a room full of other bright and successful people? How do you stand out when your accomplishments are no longer an anomaly?...You tap into your GOD given gifts! I was no longer the smartest student at the school, but I was a well-rounded individual and that is what separated me. People liked me as a person, they liked what I stood for and I built relationships where I motivated people to do something they thought they couldn't. For me, that was something to be proud of.

Whelp that was short lived. On the first day of my sophomore year, the principal was standing outside on the school steps greeting students as they came in. Although I normally took the Metro (train/bus), my mother happened to drop me off this particular day, because I was running extremely late to school. By this time, we had moved to Maryland with my Dad and my mom's new car had Maryland tags. Unbeknownst to me, the principal was not too fond of me or my mother. As I walked in the building she stopped me and asked, "Was that your mom who dropped you off?" Not thinking anything of it, I replied, "Yes," and continued through the line. Later that day my mother received a call from the school secretary, who also happened to be the staff liaison for our cheerleading team. She explained to my mom that she was instructed to investigate our residential status due to my mom's car having Maryland tags. She also brought up the fact that the principal mentioned a concern regarding my popularity at the school. I believe her exact words were, *"I've never seen a freshman who is so outspoken and knows so many upperclassmen."* Huh ***scratches head***– what does that have to do with anything? During that conversation, she mentioned that if it was determined that we did indeed reside in another state, we would be required to pay the $11,000 tuition for out of state students (***screaming - $11,000! For a FREE public school. Smh**). I couldn't help but think that yet again I was being punished for something I had no control over, and it cost me what I thought was the "perfect opportunity."

If you are going to rise, you might as well shine!

After that, I told myself - *Look, people are either going to love you or hate you and you don't have control over it one way or another.* I went on to my next school, college and career with one mission; to EXCEL. When I walked into a room, people immediately took notice, and I owned that. I listened more than I talked and I thought before I spoke, but I never apologized for my intelligence, creativity, beauty or anything else for that matter. And the few times that I slipped have turned out BAD, very BAD. Has it cost me anything? Yes! It has gotten me fired from jobs, cost me friendships that I've had since childhood, and forced me to sacrifice lots of "fun" for responsibility and structure. But would I change a thing? NO! I learned quickly that people can only see for you, what they think is possible for themselves. It's not about you. You're fighting against the insecurities they have – some they may not even know exist. So own who you are and SHINE anyway.

"They ask me where I'm moving, I say onto better things"
- Drake

Three years ago, I stepped out on faith and moved to Atlanta to reinvent myself, discover my gifts and pursue my purpose. Again, people told me I was crazy – *"You're moving to a new city, 700 miles away, by yourself?"* My answer was

ABSOLUTELY! *"Can't you do all that you're trying to do here?"* My answer was NOPE! See, during this time, I felt a major shift in my life. After my dream job turned into a complete nightmare, I decided that I would NEVER give anyone the power to control my life or my destiny again. I knew what it felt like to live a life where people felt threatened by my gifts and I was tired of shrinking to fit their mold. I had to control my success, my happiness, my influence, my name and my excellence.

I left home on a journey of discovery - everything was new to me, new city, new job, new friends and what I liked most, new possibilities. What may surprise you is that fear was not at all present. Here I was free to explore without judgment. Who cared if I failed? No one was here to point it out or be disappointed, and I liked it that way. As soon as I arrived, I began to have powerful moments of self-reflection which eventually led me to this thing called entrepreneurship. All my life I watched my family struggle and sacrifice because of money. I told myself, THAT'S IT! That is how I can truly make a difference. After tons of research, classes, tutorials and sleepless nights, I started a company called "Passions 2 Profits," now known as P2P Branded. The vision was clear, to create a company that helped the everyday man or woman take power over their lives by shining a light on their gifts, and creating a sustainable business for themselves and their families. My mom and I quickly turned this idea into a business that now helps solopreneurs and small businesses turn their unique gifts, skills and talents into innovative products and services.

From vision to execution...

Entrepreneurship is another one of those things that I've never seen successfully done first-hand. Yes, it comes with a new level of SHINE and responsibility, but the difference is that I am now up for the challenge. I get to use my light to shine a light on other people's gifts and transform the lives of those who were once in the dark. My SHINE is now appreciated and it is the catalyst that will help me to create a legacy not only for myself, but for my family. I proudly SHINE because my Success, my Happiness, my Influence, my Name and my Excellence matters!

Have you ever had a fear of standing out (SHINING)?

_____

_____

_____

What opportunities have you missed out on because you allowed someone else to dim your light?

_____

_____

If you had it your way, what would your SHINE look like to the world?

_____

_____

_____

About the Author

Jasmine Dyson began her entrepreneurial journey as a struggling college student with a need for additional income. Her basic idea was to explore her passions in a way that would generate additional income. She took her love for fashion and turned it into a business, selling jewelry and accessories. Since then, she has successfully launched 3 businesses of her own and serves as a consultant to several non-profits and business start-ups. Her educational background in management has led her to support and develop programs and initiatives for organizations in various industries. She brings a creative approach to her work that helps to expand the capacity of a company's existing framework and challenges them to explore more dynamic approaches to providing services. Over the years, she has studied and familiarized herself with cutting edge branding and design techniques, which helps her to develop more robust digital marketing and business strategies. As an avid internet and social media user herself, she speaks from an end-user's perspective and stays up on current trends in the marketplace. Her natural eye for visual presentation and industry knowledge will serve as the foundation of a great partnership between P2P Branded and your business. Learn more about Jasmine at www.crowndbyjd.com or www.p2pbranded.com.

dear fear, i am not

HER

BY MAXINE GRIFFIN SOMERVILLE :.

I Am Not Her

In Loving Memory Of Doris Graves

"A woman in harmony with her spirit is like a river flowing; she goes where she will, without pretense, and arrives at her destination prepared to be herself and only herself."

-Maya Angelou

I remember a time when I wasn't in harmony with my spirit. In fact, the word harmony was the furthest thing from my truth. Growing up, I constantly lived a life of always dimming myself, my light, who I was, to please others and to ensure their needs were met. It was only after I found myself sitting in a courtroom, defending myself against a man that I thought would love me for better or for worse, until death do us part, that I realized I was never me. I was always "HER." You know, the perfect version that everyone expects you to be? That's HER. The perfect HER. The supportive HER. The available HER. The HER solving everyone else's problems. The HER who could never say no. The understanding HER.

The "got it all together" HER. The "look at her fabulous life" HER. The HER who had to make it work for everyone else. The "no problem" HER. The "she never makes a mistake" HER. I bet there's a part of you that can relate with HER, right now (you can be honest with me).

As I sat in the courtroom that day, not knowing what the outcome would be, I realized this wasn't me, this was HER. Talk about an epiphany. On that day, my eyes were wide open! Here's what God had been telling me all along, and it took sitting in a courtroom, broken and unraveled, to hear that message loud and clear. I knew then, that it was time for me to start over again and do things for me, my way and not HER way.

At this time, I had two small children and knew in order to rebuild my life and create the life they deserved, I was going to have to serve HER an eviction notice. Was I afraid? Yes. I didn't know what this would do to me or for me. But I had to set the course for a new destination. I didn't know how I was going to get there, or even where "there" was. But I did know that she would not be present there.

How about you? How many times have you arrived at your destination where you were HER? How long have you been HER, living for others and not yourself? Isn't it exhausting? Constantly hiding your gifts because you are afraid of what others may think if you showed up as your unique self. How many times have you allowed yourself to be defined on someone else's terms, HER terms? Here's the thing about HER. She is only a title. A label given to us by others, that we have chosen to accept. And if you are anything like me, you've been living with labels for the majority of your life. But what I've learned and now can teach is that we have the power to choose!

As the oldest child, and the only girl born to my parents, my labels were reliable, conscientious, structured, unrealistic expectations, and overachieving. And my brand was the perfectionist. Some of you may be thinking, Maxine, that's not such a bad problem to have. But let me ask you something. Do you know how exhausting it is to always be expected to magically have the answers, to always be on, #nodaysoff, to never have a moment to slack? I see you shaking your head.

In choosing HER, I lost myself. This is the first time I'm admitting this; I lost me. Living up to something like perfectionism is a job that you don't want to take and one you want to leave as soon as you realize what you have signed up for. Suffering in silence became my normal. Imagine always being the person your friends called when they had a problem and the advice you gave them was the same advice you needed to give yourself. But fear convinces you that you could handle those things without help. You want to pick up the phone and send a text to someone and fear stops you dead in your tracks, the HER in your life says, "I know you are not about to do that." Always being the person when asked how are you, you say with determination and confidence, "Girl, I'm great," while the walls are falling around you. That's what life was like for me. However, because I was so afraid of what they would think, I put on my superwoman cape every day, and we (me+HER) saved the day.

My "S" quickly became heavy, stressful, and burdensome. If I knew then what I know now, there is no way I would have worn that cape. However, fear of failure is all I thought about. Who would I disappoint? Who would I fail if I was not HER? I had considered everyone else as the most important person, and the only one who really mattered...was me. The day I realized that my "S" was written in pencil, and not ink, was the most liberating moment of my life. The gig was up! And I began to erase traces of HER and truly started finding and loving me.

To be me, I mean the real me, I had to let go of who the world told me I had to be, dumping HER. That meant disappointing some people. That meant not being available all the time. That meant I had to stop hanging around people who didn't have my best interest at heart. That meant exhaling and showing up the way I needed to and not how the HER in me would have. That meant doing me the way I wanted to and not how the HER in me would. I didn't dot every "I" and cross every "T." When I did that, I started to show the world that I had the courage to let some things go. I learned to say no. I stopped desiring to "get in where I fit in" because where I was fitting in wasn't where I belonged. I need someone to really catch that right now.

To begin to reveal who I was, I had to give myself permission to let go. And right now I encourage you to do the same thing. Give yourself permission to let go of HER. Stop compensating for HER. Stop making excuses for HER. And stop fearing what life will be like when you let HER go. Give HER an expiration date today! Right now, let's do it.

On today _____ **I give myself permission**
to let HER go.
Signed,

_____

Wasn't that liberating? Don't let HER have power over you or your future. Get you back and take care of you. Practice self-love. Set realistic expectations – ones that you set for yourself and not what you think others expect of you. And just, do you.

When I began to do this, my world changed. My eyes opened. I was lighter. I was happier. I found my joy. I did things my way. I launched a business. I became an author. I became unapologetic. I found, me...the Maxine who doesn't have it all together, and that's what makes me real. I found the Maxine who doesn't have all of the answers, and that's what makes me grow more every day. I found the Maxine who isn't perfect, but has the most beautiful imperfections. I began to love me, and everything that was imperfectly me. Here are a few ways you can begin to bring the real you into your life today.

1. Identify the things you are grateful for.
2. Write those things in a gratitude journal.
3. Meditate each morning and speak authentic greatness into your day.
4. Delegate, delegate, delegate. Take off the cape and ask for help!
5. Learn to say NO. That's a one word sentence.
6. Stop feeling guilty for choosing YOU.

Reaching the "Me" elevation led to HER separation. Embrace who you are and who you want to be regardless of what others think and tell you. At the end of HER is where you will begin to live your best life. Do it with me! Take off the cape, say bye to HER, and begin to live the real you!

Why is fear keeping you attached to HER?

_____

_____

_____

What are some ways that you can begin to separate from HER today? _____

_____

_____

About the Author

Maxine Griffin Somerville is an author, speaker, consultant, career coach, and strategic professional in human resources and human capital management. Maxine has a passion for issues impacting women and families and serves as the chair of the Charles County Commission for Women where community collaboration and civic engagement are critical elements to raising awareness for women navigating life's challenges. She makes it her life's work to connect women to resources that will allow them to succeed and providing enriching experiences and opportunities for women to be their authentic selves.

Maxine holds a Bachelor of Science in Psychology from Old Dominion University and a Master of Public Administration from The George Washington University.

She is married to the love of her life, Kevin Somerville. They have five children and three grandchildren.

You can learn more about Maxine and how she can take you and your company from good to great by visiting www.enixamresources.com and following her on social media.

dear fear, you can keep your ...

TRADITIONS

BY MIKI'A PEAVY

Dear fear,

You Can Keep Your Traditions

———————————◆———————————

Here I am. Lying in bed with my tablet and my pen,
using the flashlight on my phone to keep from waking up my
ten month old son. He JUST got off my boob, by the way.
Breastfeeding days are almost over for us. I am giving the little
piranha until his first birthday, and the boobs are mine again!
Meanwhile, my fiancé' is in Chicago on an impromptu work
trip. He JUST started this job last week, so that is kind of
awesome! Our twenty-one month old son is sound asleep in his
crib downstairs, while my eighteen year old sister is able to get
her precious beauty sleep. Today was her first day of
orientation at her new job; thank God for that. Let's pause for
a second. Did I paint a vivid picture for you? This is actually a
normal night for me. A full house, being the last one up,
TRYING to feel like an adult and kid free. I should actually be
asleep myself, but I was led to pick up the pen and write at
eleven o'clock at night. So here goes…

Who am I? Well, my name is Miki'a and I am a twenty-eight year old Registered Nurse. I'm an engaged mom of two, who also helps care for my kid sister. Because my life is as non-traditional and chaotic as they come, I'm going to create a timeline for you, so try to keep up! In August of 2013, I decided to relocate from Alabama to Georgia for a better paying job. When I arrived, I arrived as single woman and no kids. I was in a relationship; however, he had made it pretty obvious over the past 4 years that he didn't want to move beyond our current stage. Atlanta was being very good to me, and by June 2014, I was all settled in and life was great. I mean, the best that it could be. The guy I was in love with (and had been in and out of a "relationship" with for almost a year) was going to be deployed soon and wanted me to start hanging out with other people. Now again, let's pause. Why is it that we, as women, KNOW when relationships are coming to a close, yet we hold on anyway? Fear! That's why. But I digress. Let's continue into my dramatic pretending that I didn't know it was over when we actually broke up at the beginning of the year.

Really? Hang out with other guys! I could not understand why he would want his "sweetheart" to be with anyone else. I simply refused! Why would I want to waste time with getting to know someone else when all I wanted was to be there for him when he returned home? But he had other plans.

And so it was. After sulking and playing the 'I don't know who I am' game, I decided to go out and make new friends. This decision led me to the most amazing and charismatic guy, or so I thought (don't judge, we've all been there). We hung out for more time than he deserved from me. I'm sure we have all had that "void" we have tried to fill. In fact, from this point on, let's call him "void filler." We had a great time and kept each other company, but eventually I realized that I wasn't *just* his good time, I was his bank! I was covering meals and dates, and one time I even had to split the bill with his mother! (Again, don't judge me, just follow the timeline). Now don't get me wrong, I don't mind treating a guy to a meal or a date, but NEVER volunteer my wallet! So yes, that amazing, charismatic guy was a complete bust.

As I sat and replayed the last year of my life, I realized that all I really wanted was to be loved. I wanted REAL LOVE. Love that never failed! Love that would fight for me when I didn't want to fight for myself. Not occasional love, or love that would be strong for a week and then the next week disappear. But it seemed as if that was my story. Every guy that I had been in love with had left me up until this point. Fear saw this as a perfect opportunity to creep in. Fear convinced me that it was me. I was the reason love didn't want to come around. I was the reason love didn't want to stay around. My mind became clouded by fear. Fear of being lonely, fear of not having someone to care about me, fear of never getting married. Fear of never becoming a mother after watching everyone close to me become mothers. I felt as if I was being punished for the decision I made in college, and I still hate to travel down that dark tunnel in my brain. Can you relate?

Christmas came and went and I was getting emails from "deployment." You know the emails that keep you hanging around but you know deep down it's not going anywhere. But that little girl in you that wants to be loved so bad wishes that it would. Yes those emails. In my head I began preparing for him to arrive in the states and we would maybe live happily ever after, together. But I was wrong...again.

In January of 2015, I was at work in the Emergency Department and at that time I didn't have a team of patients. I was floating in my pod until one of the other nurses left to go home. While I was helping everyone out, we had a young man walk in and I decided I would completely care for him since I didn't have any permanent patients at the time. I grabbed a computer and rolled it into his room. I said, "Hi, my name is Miki'a and I'm going to be taking care of you." I began to triage him and get the backstory as to why he was in the ED. He was attempting to tie up his gown in the back and I lended a helping hand. As I continued to go through his medical history, registration came into the room and asked him questions regarding his demographics and insurance.

She asked his marital status and he answered, single. I said that I understood being single because a good relationship was hard to keep. This sparked the beginning of the rest of my life. He couldn't believe I was single, a RN, and had no kids. He wanted to know if I was crazy because that had to be the ONLY reason for my marital status! As I continued to take care of him he continued to flirt. I would ask for a urine sample and he would ask for my number and a date (Seriously dude, I'm asking for urine, and you want my digits). Being the nice person I am, I just laughed it off, but he was not giving up. He eventually gave me his business card, and I took it! It turned out that he was being admitted into the hospital and as I entered the room to check on him and to give him the room number, I saw a nice looking woman. She had a long black ponytail underneath a hat and was wearing fitted workout clothes. I couldn't believe he did all of that flirting just to have a girlfriend. (Go figure, right?) When I asked him about his pain, she answered for him. He finally started to talk and introduced the woman in the room. He said, "This is my mom and she's a Delta like you." His MOM! (Okay, maybe I wrote him off too soon.)

That morning after I got home from work, I started removing junk out of my scrub pockets and there was his business card. I grabbed my phone and shot him a quick text and he instantly replied. Usually I wouldn't do anything like this, however, I thought what's the worst that can happen. We talked a little while longer and then I had to rest for work that same night. I didn't want to jinx anything, but he was a really nice guy. The nights I worked that week, I would take a trip upstairs during my break to visit him. We talked as if we had known each other for years. He had an awesome smile and dreamy eyes; I wanted to make sure I wasn't gazing too much. After working my last shift for the week, I decided to buy the two of us Waffle House. I went back to the hospital for another hour and had breakfast with him. He was really surprised and insisted on paying me back. I refused to accept but he somehow snuck twenty-dollars in my coat pocket after I hugged him good-bye. He was finally discharged from the hospital six days later and asked to take me to breakfast after I got off work the next morning. I agreed, but I was super late (45 minutes) after being held up at a uniform sale at work. He never complained, but joked about telling the waitress that he was not being stood up by a date! After our IHOP breakfast, the rest was history. We spent every day together. Dates, texting, talking on the phone- you name it. We talked about our past relationships and I gave him many details about "deployment" and how I planned on being there once his ship returned to the states.(Yes, I know. You can say it). However, once I officially confirmed with "deployment" that we were no longer and would never be an item, I was open to all possibilities with my new friend.

We both decided that we needed a vacation and planned a trip to go to New Orleans the weekend after Mardi Gras. The hotel had complimentary wine and red beans and rice with the sweetest cornbread I ever had. I had a couple of glasses of wine and maybe a cocktail. We fully took advantage of that perk. So much that a month later, I soon found out that we would be parents! I told you all to keep up!

I didn't think I would ever be this happy again. I was on Cloud 9! We had both fallen deep for each other. We weren't afraid of parenthood, but afraid of others opinion of us. We were living our life truly untraditional. What would they say? What would they think? Would we be disowned? Yes we were grown, but let's be honest, when you have living parents and grandparents, are we ever grown enough to go against the grain? Time passed by, and we went from continuing to learn who the other person was to learning how to be parents. No we weren't married and neither had we been dating for years! We didn't have a house, but were still renting. Let's just say tradition had been kicked out of our relationship from the very beginning. After the months passed, many obstacles had been thrown our way. We began having relationship problems and then we gave birth to our son eight weeks early. As if that wasn't enough, four months passed and we found out I was pregnant again. This time I wasn't happy. I cried ironically like the newborn baby I already had! Things changed again. Now we were finding a home to fit all of us. We had to think differently financially because here was another blessing but also another mouth to feed. The worst thing that still pulls at my heart is losing the loan to the house that we saw start from the ground up. We chose everything to make this the perfect home for our growing family, from the outside paint to the shiny- rainbow tinted knobs on the cabinets. All the hard work went to waste. Our closing date was two weeks before I went on early maternity leave for our second son. TWO WEEKS and just like that our dream was torn away. I was afraid that I was failing at life. Fear told me it's because you wanted love so bad, look what love does. I knew that if I wanted to have a successful home and raise 2 amazing young men that I would have to let go of the self-doubt, worry, pity and fear and trust God. The road hasn't been easy and I have gone from being a super nurse (and super single) to being a super mom (and engaged). Every day my story is still being written, but I am the one that gets to tell it. Not fear. Fear tried to submit me to old traditions, but DEAR FEAR: YOU CAN KEEP YOUR OLD TRADITIONS; I'M CREATING MY OWN.

Now it's your turn. Use this area to tell fear you are creating your own traditions. Whether that's your career, life, business, family, marriage...it's YOUR life. And no one else can tell you how to live it.

About the Author

Miki'a Peavy, BSN, RN has always had a passion for helping others, leading her into the medical field. As a 2011 graduate of Stillman College, Miki'a held the third highest GPA in her nursing class. Miki'a is first a mother to her boys, Grayson and August, and then a nurse. She continues to push through her fears and be the best she can be in faith, parenting, love and her career. Throughout the ups and downs, she has been able to stay afloat and continues to try and make love work. If you would like to follow her life and interact with her throughout her blogging journey then head over to mikiashae.wordpress.com.

Dear fear, I am not a slave to you, I am not shackled to you, we are not bound together, and I can leave you whenever I need to. I understand your presence is there and I understand your presence is probably needed because without fear I can't have strength and courage. Fear I acknowledge you are there but I understand you are completely replaceable and I can completely get rid of you and I am not bound to you or your motives.

Amber Aziza
www.asquaredcoach.com

BREAKING

BY ANNA MOSBY

dear fear, you can't take my ...

Dear fear,

You Can't Take My Breaking

◆————————————————————————◆

"Oh, Anna, I don't know how you do it."
"I would be scared to death, but you handle everything and just seem to be fine."
"I wish I had your strength."
"I know it's difficult, but I know you, so I know you've got it under control; you always do."

Those were just some of the many "encouraging" comments I received in the midst of one of the darkest periods in my life. I would smile and sincerely say, "thank you", but honestly, many times, I was breaking inside. Every day, and especially on Sunday morning, I would put on my makeup, both physically and emotionally, and face the world as if everything was fine. Sunday mornings were sometimes the worst.

It literally was "the best of times and the worst of times." Things had been going very well – not perfect, but I could truly say that I was blessed. My family was great, providing unconditional love and support for my busy lifestyle. My ministry was going well. As an ordained minister in the African Methodist Episcopal (A.M.E.) Church, I was preaching, teaching, and actively leading. As the Minister to Women in my local church, I coordinated weekend retreats, facilitated workshops and provided individual counseling and comfort to hundreds of women. My mission was to empower women (and men) to excel and lead through the power of Jesus Christ. I also led a financial literacy ministry utilizing my training and experience. Many would have called me successful. And by the world's standards, I was. In addition to God's calling to ordained ministry, I worked full time for a national consulting firm, holding the title "Vice President." I was responsible for managing multi-million dollar projects and was blessed with a six-figure salary. Again, things were going well. But then the phone call came. Yes, the dreadful call that initiated my drop into what felt like the worst of times. My entire division was eliminated and I was RIF'd – the victim of a Reduction in Force.

Once the shock wore off, I moved quickly to look for another position. While I wasn't naive enough to think it would be "easy," I did expect something to happen relatively soon. After all, I was "successful." I was armed with Master of Business Administration (MBA) and Master of Divinity (MDiv) degrees, and years of experience as an Investment

Manager, Project Manager and national Vice President; of course someone would hire me. But, days turned into weeks and weeks turned into months. My savings dwindled; I was forced to tap into my retirement account; and still, no job.

Through this journey, my faith was stretched, tested and strengthened. Why would God allow this to happen to me?! What had I done wrong? I asked all the cliché questions that I already knew the answers to.

You see what we often see as punishment is really God pruning us for the promotion He has in store for us.

While I'm great at preaching to everyone else, it was in this season that I was suddenly forced to truly hear my own words.

Sundays were the worst. In the middle of my season of unemployment, I received my first Pastoral appointment. I was a Pastor! I experienced the full range of emotions, all of which were positive (until Fear came around). This is what I had been praying and preparing for, to use my leadership and ministry gifts. But the reality is, first appointments are proving ground for promotion. It is seldom that one is given a large church, large congregation and large salary the first time. So now I had a salary, but not enough to survive on – or so I thought.

Sundays were the worst. Having spent time with the Lord all week, praying, meditating, preparing my sermon, I would make the one-hour drive to church and realize I was not in the car alone. FEAR was riding in the passenger seat. FEAR was sitting in the back. FEAR was harmonizing with every gospel song played on the radio. Every song of encouragement caused me to cry out to God – "How much longer?!" But by the time I arrived at church, I had prayed prayers of faith, wiped away the tears, reapplied my mascara, and was ready to encourage my congregation. Understand, this is not to say I did not trust God or believe God would see me through and even carry me through. I saw God making a way; I saw God providing all of my needs and many of my wants. I felt God's protection and loving embrace. My point is, Fear only needs a window or a small opening to push its way in and bring doubt and depression along with it. When you find yourself in a season of brokenness, know that faith is the only sure weapon against fear.

Sundays were the worst. But Sundays were also the best! I learned to embrace and use every opportunity, every day and every moment, to glorify God while going through. I call it a "yet" praise – you haven't seen the solution … yet, but thank God now. You haven't witnessed the healing … yet, but thank God now. You haven't been restored … yet, but go ahead and put a down payment on your miracle now. When you are able to do that, Sundays, and every day, become the best!

It was in the midst of my "yet" praise that I was reminded, it wasn't the situation that needed to be changed, it was me. Seasons of brokenness are for a reason. What was God challenging me to do? What were the lessons I needed to learn? I prayed that I would see the blessings even in the midst of my brokenness. And it was then that I was led to start my own consulting firm. It was then, in the midst of my brokenness, that my blessings began to rain down. It was then that my "yet" praise became my best praise! I realized that God had to retire me from ordinary in order to get to extraordinary! There is something liberating about embracing and implementing your own vision. I realized that I was born to lead. And in that moment, I declared that I was done following Fear.

Here's what I have learned. If you are willing to take chances, take advantage of opportunities, and step out of your comfort zone, God will open unexpected doors and take you places you never anticipated or imagined. I've been blessed to travel, speak, teach and preach across the country, in the Caribbean, the Bahamas, Egypt, Israel, and West Africa. Even more important than the locale, is the people I've met, and the difference I've made in their lives and they've made in mine. Every opportunity, every experience, every trial and test, every failure and success is a reminder of what can happen when we refuse to allow fear to take control. After three years of "under employment" my season of testing was over – wait, let me be clear. THAT season of testing was over (there are always more). As things turned around, I took time to reflect on what I had learned. I now take these lessons with me as I navigate through new seasons of challenge and growth, and I use them to teach others.

First of all, I was reminded that brokenness builds confidence. Fear will divert your attention from who you are and what you've accomplished. When the job offers did not come flooding in, I began to doubt my abilities and question my qualifications. But when I saw my broken situation as an opportunity for a new beginning, I started my own business. As I developed my marketing plan and described who I was and what I had to offer, I was personally empowered and declared that Fear is a liar; Fear does not know me, does not own me and cannot define me. My challenge to you – don't let Fear define or discourage you.

Secondly, I learned, again, that effective leadership comes with the freedom and responsibility to speak God's truth to every situation. Effective leaders do not let Fear keep them from speaking against injustice. Never lose your unique voice. Everyday each of us is faced with situations that require a choice, speak up or remain silent. Sometimes, it is not worth the drama, it's just not that important. But when you are faced with a situation that demands a response, don't let fear keep you from taking a stand. Don't buy into the negative narrative that labels women as aggressive and abrasive and men as assertive and authoritative. These descriptors have no gender and can be appropriate or inappropriate, depending on the situation and setting. I am also a firm believer that everyone needs a battle scripture, that affirming Word you can declare in the midst of whatever you are going through. "I can do all things through Christ who strengthens me." "Greater is He that is in me than he that is in the world." "I shall not die but live, and declare the works of the Lord." What is your battle scripture?

Finally, perhaps the most important lesson I've learned. is that at the end of the day, it's not about you. It's about how your experiences can help someone else. You were created to lead. Be sure you know where you are going and identify the steps required to successfully get there. Leadership means creating and embracing your vision, then writing and rewriting long- and short-term goals necessary to get you there. Leading forward toward your fabulous future means not only self-empowerment, but empowering those who will walk with you and follow in your path. Someone is watching and learning from your lead.

One of the most important things we can do is leave a legacy impression that ensures our footprint is impactful and makes a difference in someone's life. I was amazed how many people took time to tell me what a difference I've made in their lives by encouraging them and reminding them how special, gifted, creative, and necessary they are. I was leading, just by fighting fear. I was leading by pressing through my own brokenness and helping someone else through hers. I didn't just come through, I brought others through; I reached back and grabbed others to keep them from being left behind and left out and lost.

Brokenness is a part of life. The question is, what do we do with the broken pieces? Do we sit in the middle of them and cry or do we sweep them aside and move forward? Do we allow the walls of sexism and racism and gender bias to block our blessings or do we break through and break out? God heals the broken hearted and binds up their wounds (Psalm 147:3), so I encourage you to break through. Break the glass ceiling. Break the mold. Break the cycle. Break the generational curse. There is beauty in your brokenness. Break through and press to the other side. If you feel like you are drowning, swim, tread water or just hold on to the broken pieces of the ship, but don't give up until you get through to the other side. Ride the waves of doubt, the waves of fear, and the waves of uncertainty.

If you are in a desert place, an uncomfortable and lonely place, keep walking until you get through the desert. Find an oasis of quiet refreshing, then start moving again. Don't get distracted or discouraged. Fear will tell you it's too late. Fear will tell you that you'll never make it, never succeed, and maybe not even survive. Fear's assignment is to divert and detour you from your divine destiny, but if you continue to walk **through**, not only will you find joy along the journey but you will discover that Fear cannot take your brokenness. Fear cannot win. You were born to lead. Whether you want to be CEO of a large organization, CEO of your own business enterprise, or CEO of your life, it's time to lead with confidence, free from fear and with an eye on the future. Fear cannot win and Fear cannot take your brokenness. Break through and soar! Declare it – Dear Fear, You Can NOT Take My Breaking!

What are some areas of your life where you feel or may have felt broken?

_____

_____

_____

What have you learned that you can use to reach back and pull someone else forward?

_____

_____

_____

Anna Mosby has a passion for empowering and encouraging women to be everything God created them to be. She is a Pastor, Preacher, Speaker, Leadership Coach and the Founder of Anna Mosby Consulting. Anna guides women as they find their authentic and awesome selves using her proven approach – The 3F Leadership Model. Reverend Anna is multi-vocational and active in church and community. She currently serves as the Senior Pastor of St. Jude A.M.E. Church in Germantown, Maryland as well as the President of the 2nd Episcopal District Women in Ministry, providing leadership to over 900 female clergy serving in A.M.E. churches across Maryland, Virginia, North Carolina and the District of Columbia. She is also a member of Delta Sigma Theta Sorority, Inc. Anna holds a Bachelor of Business Administration, with a concentration in Finance, a Master of Business Administration and a Master of Divinity. Learn more at www.annamosby.com.

STORY

BY KINDRA WHITNEY TRAWICK

dear fear, you can't have any...

You Can't Have My Story

◆————————————————————————————————————◆

"God, please don't take my mom. Just tell me what you want
me to do, I'll do it. But please don't take her."

I remember sitting at the hospital praying and asking
God to allow my mother to stay on Earth. As I stood over her,
watching the machines assisting her to live, I began praying
that she would fight and stay with me a little longer. The tears
began to fall without warning and I couldn't stop the flow. I
had never felt so helpless. Just a few minutes prior, she and I
were talking. She was encouraging me and telling me that I
was going to make it and be successful in life. She smiled and
told me how proud she was of me, and how in her mind I was
already a star. Within moments, nurses rushed in, and now...we
were here.

I took my time praying over my mother, from the top
of her head to the soles of her feet. I couldn't imagine a world
without her in it, but when the visitation hours were over, I

kissed my mom and walked out knowing that God would have the final say. Shortly after I left the hospital, I received a call. I knew that it wasn't good. When I returned the call, I was informed that my mom had passed away. Fear immediately attached itself to me. Fear told me that I couldn't go on without my mother. "First your grandmother, and now your mother Kindra?" Fear convinced me that I was no longer needed. Fear showered me with doubt, depression and confusion. But mostly, fear made me believe that what my mother saw in me would never come to pass. I realized that I needed to break up with fear in order to live out my destiny. I told God that I trusted him, and surrendered to HIS will, not fears. And I grabbed a pen, and I wrote:

Dear Fear,

I am probably the last person you expected to hear from, being that you had such a hold on me at one point in time. I bet you thought I'd never leave. I am writing this letter with a smile, which is something I haven't done in a while. I have something I have to get off my chest, and now I know that this is for the best. You had me in such a dark and faithless place, I couldn't stand to look in the mirror to see my own face. My identity you took from me, without a trace, but I realized you were more like lead, not ink, so you could be erased. I remember the times you had me afraid of EVERTHING! For

30 years you held me in bondage, but facing you is my key to freedom. I know you have been lurking, waiting to get in where you fit in; however, it's OVER BOO! I would never give you another chance, and even if I saw you again I wouldn't give you a second glance. Fear, I will admit you are a smooth criminal. The way you crept in, swept me off my feet, and made me fall so hard for you. Your sweet whispers and warm embrace were fulfilling, and I wasn't reluctant but willing, to give you a place to stay and feed you too! You had me thinking you were the best thing on this side of heaven and that you were protecting me from being hurt. The dates with you were endless and the passion you had for me had me thinking about marriage. Yes, I was ready to say "I do" to you. Pledging my undying love to your protection from my purpose. I found comfort in knowing that if I had no one else, you would be there, keeping me safe from my destiny of being great. You were my best friend. I told you my secrets during pillow talk, and in turn you reminded me of the rejection I experienced in the past, closing my eyes from the potential of a brighter future. You were there when no one else could be found, so I became fond of your presence. Your presence soothed me. Until one night, I woke up, and I knew something wasn't right. I couldn't rest and my intuition was relentless. I prayed and asked God to show me your true intentions, and some things that were shown, I would rather not mention. I got

up and packed your things and set them on fire like the scene in Waiting To Exhale, because the doubt, insecurities, and overwhelm that you instilled in me were trash. So fear, I am writing you this letter in case you did not get the memo. We are over. And you are no longer welcome. My life has begun. And your season is no more. I will make it my mission to warn every woman of your manipulative ways, with your cunning acts and sickening embrace. I am grateful for our experience because without it I would have never been introduced to my new boo, FAITH! Yes, I now walk in faith, and I've learned to walk without fear. The very thing you kept me from seeking is the very thing God is blessing me with. And I've never been happier. You can't have my story fear...or my faith.

Sincerely Your EX,

Kindra Whitney Trawick

Kindra Whitney Trawick is a native of Newark, New Jersey and a resident of Dothan, Alabama. She has always had a passion for inspiring, motivating, and uplifting people, whether it's through comedy, emceeing, speaking, vlogging, or writing. She is currently completing her first book titled "PainKillers." She is the host of a weekly blog, JustKindra, and an annual symposium, "Reaching For The Future." Her work has been featured on several news outlets, including Fox 34. Kindra's purpose is to push people past pain, get people to acknowledge God in everything, and know that they are important. She is Just Living, Just Loving, Just Learning...JustKindra. Follow her on Facebook, Instagram and Snapchat at IAmJustKindra.

DREAM

BY MONICA BOYD

dear fear, you can't have my ...

Dear fear,

You Can't Have My Dream

◆————————————————————————————◆

My purpose in sharing my journey with you is to unlock a voice that's been silent waaay too long. And by doing so, hopefully, I can help you move from your comfort zone into your next season…the season that you deserve on the other side of fear.

I grew up in a time when children were raised to be seen and *not heard.* I grew up in a time when children were not allowed to listen in on "grown folks" conversation. I grew up in a time when "what goes on in this house, stays in this house." As a child, I was the invisible witness to frequent domestic abuse. As a child, I couldn't understand why the person being abused didn't fight the attacker back. "Attacker" is a strong word, but in my 6 year old mind, that's what it was. . . an attack. And while I had no voice in the matter, it is THE reason I have zero tolerance for domestic abuse today.

I went to parochial school from kindergarten through high school. This was a time when priests wore clerical collars and nuns wore habits (think penguin, Whoopie Goldberg, Sister Act). Sister Mary didn't think twice about whacking you across the knuckles with a wooden ruler or your bottom with a wooden paddle! I had no voice, only rules to follow. From grade school to high school, there was always the spoken and unspoken rules *to be quiet*. To behave. To follow the rules. To always ask permission. Nothing wrong with structure, EXCEPT when structure interferes with your creativity and your purpose. (Great artists did not become great by painting inside the lines; think about that). School was always structured and predictable, while home was anything but. So I had to quickly learn how to navigate two very different worlds: one I loved and one I dreaded. During my middle school years, I escaped reality through books (to this day, I prefer a good book over most other activity). By high school, I began to seriously imagine myself in a different place, living a more ideal life. Don't get me wrong, while my childhood was not idyllic, there were plenty of fun times! To this day, I still laugh about some of those times! But there were also experiences that caused much pain, and I choose to remain quiet about some of them. I have forgiven others, but it has taken so much longer to forgive myself so I can heal and move forward in my purpose. There is very little I would change, even the hard stuff. Because it's the hard stuff that made me the resilient person I am today. I graduated high school in 3 years instead of the traditional four, because I was very eager to start living the life I dreamed about. Big city. High rise apartment. Medical school. Lots of money for traveling and fancy cars, buying things I *wanted* instead of only what I *needed*. Nothing was going to tie me down – no kids, no husband, nothing! Finally, after so many years of taking care of other people, I could concentrate on just me and a job that I loved! New York City was calling my name. However, without proper guidance, I didn't have a well thought out plan, so that dream never became my reality. After high school, I went to state university (age 16) for one year. But without proper planning, all that daydreaming had to come to a halt. I didn't have money to finish college, so I had to get a job. Shortly thereafter, I got pregnant. And while I actually enjoyed being pregnant, I was right where I didn't want to be; responsible for another life!

I went on to the proverbial Corporate America and was introduced to yet another set of rules to obey. These rules ultimately reinforced that I had no voice. You really don't want to rock the boat here! You've got babies to feed. A mortgage. A car note. Diapers. Formula. Daycare. College will be here before you know it. Fear set in quickly, and I became voiceless and submissive. For several years, I was in a sandwich generation – children young enough to still need me and an aging parent. I had to ration vacation days to accommodate both. So, there was never any opportunity for ME to take vacation days to rest and recharge. Mental health days were far and few between. And the more silent I became, the more needed those days were. It was hard for me to have a real voice on the job. I needed that job! Fear convinced me to silence my *real* opinions when my manager asked me for my thoughts. I realized I had two options (in reality, my fear only gave me two options): silence (my first choice) or just agree. Why should I waste my good mental energy, giving my real opinion, when I KNOW management is not even remotely interested in a voice different from theirs? And since I'm not into brown nosing (couldn't think of a nicer way to say that and capture the essence of what I meant), I just kept quiet. I wish I could tell you how many times that quietness got me in trouble. This was one of those, 'I can't win for losing' situations. If I agreed, I got reprimanded on the performance review for bringing nothing new to the table. If I disagreed, I got reprimanded for not being. . . get this. . . A TEAM PLAYER. What? How I learned to hate that annual performance review!

My self-esteem always took a hit after the discussion phase. Mostly because the very thing I got dinged for, a colleague would do, and seemingly got rewarded for it. Or, at least NOT reprimanded. Hmmm! **It would be years before I realized that piece of paper DID NOT define who I was!**

That revelation was a clear turning point for me. From that point forward, I started to think differently about myself and cared absolutely zero about that stupid performance review. I still maintained my silence but it was a different kind of silence. I had a voice, but "I" chose not to use it. Now, that I had reclaimed my voice, I had to formulate a plan to reclaim my time, and that plan started with targeted prayers and the Word of God!

The main lesson I learned from all of these shenanigans is this; management had low self-esteem. Anytime you're the manager and you can't be mature enough to at least hear a viewpoint different from your own, there are deeper issues at work. I share this not to degrade another person or make myself look like a hero, but because I know how frustrating a job can be, especially when it is NOT helping you achieve your dreams. Rather you are promoting someone else's dreams and building their bank account. I share to help YOU understand, if you are still working a 9 to 5, please understand management has lots going on in their personal and professional lives. What I've learned about people that must always have things their way, is this: they generally have low self-esteem; they often do not have a voice at home; they are almost always dealing with a personal issue (pending divorce, unruly child(ren), sick parent, upper management riding his/her back), the list goes on. What I wish I knew then was, I had done nothing wrong EXCEPT put someone else's feelings ahead of my own (Women are good at this.) I had allowed someone else to project their low self-esteem mindset onto me. I also realized, after the fact, my season in that position was over! Why did I stay so long? Why did I allow myself to be so miserable day in and day out? Crying on my drive to work (didn't want to go). Crying on the drive home from work (because I continued to give my all, only to be told it wasn't enough). I was not being heard or valued! It was comfortable financially, but it was costing me everywhere else. I had become numb to my dreams. That season taught me that you should always work in a place where your ideas are accepted and you are celebrated. If this is not where you are, start looking! It doesn't have to be an immediate career move, but you need to be formulating a plan and that plan needs to start with prayer. Don't be afraid to seek God's guidance in the professional workplaces.

Up until now, I THOUGHT I was trusting God. I had a wonderful family and I had built the life I wanted. But still, something was missing, and it wasn't just needing a new job. I needed a new direction! So, I started to pray very specific prayers. I was very vulnerable with God. Repentant. Apologetic. Transparent. It was then that I realized, not having a voice, not being heard, had a heavier impact on me than I thought. I realized, I was depressed. *Me? I couldn't be.* But I was. I was beyond ready for a new direction. I was miserable. I was down in the dumps. I was unhappy. My energy level was so low. There was some days, it was all I could do to pull myself out of bed to shower and eat. And trust me, this girl likes to eat! Remember, I was praying for God to give me new direction. You don't just leave a job after 36+ years without a plan. I remembered from years ago, I didn't have a full plan from high school forward and that fell flat in a year. But all the while I was praying, God never gave me permission to leave the job. What He did, was reorganized the division I was in so that I was 'severed'. Through corporate restructuring, my division was relocated and I was without a job. I cried all the way home – tears of joy! God had answered my prayer for a new direction. Sounds glam, but it was at this point that FEAR really set in. I'd had a career routine for a lifetime. Now all of a sudden, I didn't. There was no reason to get up in the morning. I could sleep as long as I wanted. Watch as much TV as I wanted. But truth be told, I floundered without the routine of the previous 36 years. And while I was going from mild panic to frantic, God gently reminded me, this was the new season I had prayed for. Oh! That part I liked. Sounded real good when I had a steady paycheck. But the uncertainty of not knowing how things were going to turn out, I certainly DID NOT like! I felt like Moses. I knew God had spoken to me. I knew HE had a plan for me (Jer 29:11). I knew I'd be alright and He'd make sure I had victory (2 Cor 2:14). It's one thing to read a finished account in the bible. It's another thing to walk it out when you don't know the steps in between.

During this season, I had to learn to trust God. For the very first time, "I" was F.R.E.E. to choose. I mean REALLY choose. I have to admit, I struggled at first because I was so used to everybody else telling me what to do, when to do it, how to do it. I was so busy trying not to rock the boat that it took years for me to realize, *my life looked nothing like my dreams.* But as God would have it, the very first manager He connected me with on my new journey said words to me during the interview that I will NEVER forget. (To help you understand my position, you had to know I was nervous to interview after 36+ years. I was on the wrong side of the desk. I was used to being the hiring manager, not looking to get hired.) Anyway, after reviewing my resume, experience, and credentials, he stood up from his seat behind the desk, looked me straight in the eyes and with all sincerity said to me, *"You don't need to be employed, you need to be empowered."* Thanks David B! You have no idea the profound impact those words had (another critical turning point). Those simple words *released me* to walk into my purpose. I can tell you, those words spoke life to me. Proverbs 18:21, says, "Death and life are in the power of the tongue." The Word never said it had to be MY tongue. So in that moment, after years of having my dreams and purpose and destiny suppressed, I was released to move forward. In that moment, I realized those dreams I had could be dusted off and revived. In that moment, I realized it was NOT too late to chase my dream. In that moment, there was a refreshing that my words cannot adequately describe. If you have ever had those 'life giving' words spoken to you by a person or by God Himself, then you know what I'm describing. If that hasn't happened to you yet, and you have still been suppressing your dreams and you are frozen due to fear, 'wait I say, on the Lord' (Psalm 27:14). What I didn't know then, is that it would take another few years for me to work through my fear. All those years of being silent had finally taken its toll. Fear had ultimately taken my voice. I was no longer fierce, I was frozen. I didn't trust people, especially those in position of authority. Fear stole opportunities and cost me money. And let me say this, I'm not sure fear ever goes away *completely*. But the more you conquer it, the smaller it becomes. But fast forward from 2014 to 2017.

In January 2017, I still remember clearly praying for God to connect me to people that would help me fulfill my dream. I had to be raw and honest and ask God to help me trust again. Not just trust Him, but trust people. God responded by connecting me to the most amazing individuals; Ethel Davis, Linda Clemons and Tiana Patrice, to name a few. From January 2017 until the writing of this book, I have been blessed to receive encouragement and mentoring from the best of the best – because you certainly cannot do it alone. Seek professional connections that will take you to the next level. Don't be afraid to invest in yourself – time and money. Take the time you need to heal so you can offer your best, authentic self to others.

I almost forgot, in 2002, I wrote a proposal to my corporate managers at the time. It was an idea to generate revenue for the firm and fill an important void. Most managers agreed it was a good idea but the final voice said NO. I was crushed. There was no way for me to know in 2002, that in 2017, I would form and become the President of a financial education company, be an international speaker, and host my own successful conferences! The proposal that man rejected in 2002, God approved in 2017! Fear Less! After all these years of fulfilling other people's dreams, I can now boldly say: DEAR FEAR, YOU CAN'T HAVE MY DREAM!

How have you allowed fear to take your dream?

_____

_____

_____

What would you do if only you weren't afraid?

_____

_____

_____

About the Author

Monica Boyd is the founder of I Am Wealth Builders, which was founded in 2017. After spending more than 40 years in the corporate financial arena, Monica decided to take her experience and build her own dreams. She now helps struggling and frustrated women leaders build generational wealth and make their money last. You can learn more about Monica at www.monicadboyd.com, and take her FREE 5 day course, Make Your Money Last. Monica is married to her high school sweetheart. They have two adult children and 7 grandchildren.

GREATNESS

BY NEECEE TOMAS

dear fear, you can't have my ...

Dear fear,

You Can't Have My Greatness

◆————————————————————————————————◆

Have you heard the old saying, _If I knew back then what I know now_? Well I'll tell you, that statement has a lot of truth to it. I'm sure you're shaking your head in agreement right now. When I look back through the various stages of my life, I cringe sometimes. I recognize how lonely and afraid I really was. The crazy part? I didn't realize it; we seldom do. In my mind, I was brave. I thought because I had a lot of mouth, i.e. the gift of gab, that meant that I was smart, courageous, bold and confident, but in reality, I was really scared. I had no direction. I was just living life on my own, leaning to my own understanding, doing what I thought was best for me at any given moment. I didn't realize how my decisions would impact me throughout these various stages of my life. Before I get too deep into my story, let me tell you a little bit about me.

My name is Denise, NeeCee for short. I'm the product of a single-parent home. My mom raised me, and 2 of my 3 siblings by herself. I am one of the middle children of 4. My mom has been the only constant in my life for me to glean from, but she was limited by her environment and exposure. Nevertheless, she was the only example I knew to follow at the time. We didn't know it then, but we are all products of our environment. I would venture to say that if she had to do it all over again, there would be a few things she would change as well. I saw my mom go to work and make great sacrifices to ensure that me and my siblings had all of our needs met. I didn't say that we had everything we wanted, but we never knew lack.

Unlike my mom, I became a mom at the age of 16. The 9th grade was the last year I completed in school. I never went back to school after that, instead within a few years I started studying for my G.E.D. I successfully passed the test during the same timeframe I would have graduated high school. Being a teen mom had its own challenges, after all I was still a child myself. I didn't know the first thing about being anybody's parent, except what I saw in my environment. I had my son at 16, and I was living on my own by the time I was 18 years of age. I realized that having a baby and living on your own doesn't make you grown, but it will surely grow you up real fast. My mom wasn't one of those moms who took care of the baby while I lived my life. On the contrary, she made it really clear that Darren was my baby and it was my responsibility to take care of him. Although she helped me out, she made sure that I didn't get my role mixed up with hers.

When I started working for the Federal Government in 1984, at the ripe age of 19, I was like a fish out of water. I had no clue about career development or planning. I had no goals or aspirations. The thought never occurred to me that there was a career path I could follow to progressively move me up. I was clueless. All I knew was that I was working for the Federal Government, and that meant something to me in terms of being able to provide for my son and get off of public assistance. After about 10 years in my job, I started to get clued in to the changes happening in my environment. When I first started working, the majority of the folks working with me were just like me; clueless about our direction in life, let alone our careers. As more of the change in my work environment started happening, I began to develop a hunger and thirst for more, but I still wasn't sure what it all meant at the time. I knew my job very well, as a matter of fact I was one of the "go-to" people. I have always been a quick learner, so I stood out amongst my peers. Over a period of time, more and more opportunities started opening up for advancement. I was selected for an upward mobility program which put me on an accelerated track. Before I knew it, I was at the top of the chart. To move up further at that time, I would have to become a supervisor. Yep, you guessed it, that door opened too. It was a temporary position for 2 years, but I had the opportunity to be selected for the permanent position at the end of the 2 years. After the 2 years, I just knew that I was going to be automatically selected for the position. Guess what, not only was I not selected. I didn't even get an interview or an acknowledgement that I had applied for the position. Yikes, what in the world! After all, I was the cream of the crop, I was the go-to person. What happened? I was hurt, confused and crushed. That's when I started looking at myself; no, that's a lie, I started telling myself that it was them and not me; that they were prejudiced or that they didn't like people who spoke up; they just wanted a "yes man." it sounded like a good enough reason to me. It was not until I got passed over the second time that I started to look at me. At this point, I am about 15 years into my career. When I started to take inventory, I had to admit that the credentials that the others brought to the table shined more brightly than mine; besides, I was loud, outspoken and had not yet learned how to hold my tongue. If I saw it as an injustice, I would be the first one to speak up and spoke for everybody else too, not yet realizing that the others must have known better. Somebody had obviously clued them in about avoiding career suicide. It's okay to think it, but not always okay to say it. Mind you, these are people who worked closely with me. I even considered a few of them my friends. They listened to me rant and rag on my supervisor, even being insubordinate at times. They were the ones that got selected for the positions I got passed over for.

What is the point of telling you all of this? I'm glad you asked. It matters how you start out. It matters what information you have, and environment plays a huge role in how we progress in life. Through a series of events, some more painful than others, I would come to realize that God had a plan for my life all along, but in the meantime, it still didn't make a whole lot of sense to me personally. I wish I could tell you that once I had an encounter with God, my eyes opened and my career just took off and that everything was happily ever after. Nope, quite the contrary. During this period in my life, I recall that I thought I knew everything that I needed to know about life, so a life coach was the furthest thing from my mind and mentors were not a buzzword used in my circles. I didn't realize it at the time, but I started sinking into depression, nothing seemed to be going right. I was not successful at home or work; I was going through the motions, no dreams, no goals, no visions, just existing, just surviving. I remember thinking that this is what it's all about, working, having fun, then dying, and that the emotions I was experiencing was normal. It was a vicious never-ending cycle. I didn't realize it then, but I was settling. Whatever happened in life, I settled for it. I didn't have to explain anything to anybody, and nobody was asking me any questions. After I got passed over for those 2 promotions, I stopped trying. Fear convinced me that I wasn't good enough. I fell back, and that outspoken woman became quiet. My confidence was gone.

It was not until I had a noticeable encounter with God that I started to pay attention. That is when I started to realize how frightened I really was and how much being passed over affected me in my personal life as well as my professional life. It took me years to regain my voice. After I started experiencing God in a more personal way, He started showing me the errors of my ways and what had really happened when I had been passed over. He showed me how I could have royally jacked up some folks' lives if I was chosen as their leader. He showed me that I wasn't ready; I wasn't yet qualified to take on that responsibility. This is when I learned that it matters very little to most people what you know. If you do not fit into their ideal plan, you can be smart as you want to be, but they do not have to select you.

While I was starting to develop my personal relationship with God, I still didn't have confidence in my ability. I still had it ingrained in me that I wasn't good enough, that I wasn't smart enough to sit at the table with my peers. This held me back in my career. I wanted to stay in the background; it was safe there. I didn't have to be afraid that someone would judge me or that I would use words in the wrong context, or that I would stumble over my words or that I didn't have anything relevant to contribute to the conversation. In my mind, the lack of education, personal growth, and development said that I better keep quiet before they find me out.

One of my turning points came when my deputy director told me that she wanted me to be the face of my division. Not only did I turn down the position, but I became very adamant with her that it wasn't for me. The truth of the matter is, I didn't know what "face of the division" meant, or what it looked like. I was afraid to tell her that. I was afraid for people to know that I did not know. Slowly but surely, the message of what she was conveying to me started to sink in and I embraced the challenge to become the face of my division. I remember one day having an ah-ha moment, as if the lights suddenly came on for me. And so, my journey began.

During this time, I had grown a bit more in my relationship with God, in that I could hear him better. I sensed Him urging me to wake up and begin to get me in order for the blessings he had for me. Now that my eyes are open, and I began to push beyond my fear, I am writing to you at 30 years into my career. I came in with no plan or vision for my life, but now I sit at the top of the GS scale. All praise to God, because I told you that I had my first child at 16. I dropped out of school, got a G.E.D, didn't go to college. I could have easily been fired within the first 3 years. I was loud, outspoken, and didn't miss an opportunity to tell somebody how I felt. But God saw favor in me. And as he prepared me, he continued to position me for my next.

As I come to the end of my chapter, allow me to summarize everything I just said. Environment plays a huge role in how we progress in life. The people that we allow to speak into our lives is huge. The things and people we listen to and watch, up close or from afar play a huge role in our lives. Spending time with God and through the awesome teaching of my church, I began to get a clearer vision of the impact and significance of my life. My life is not just about me, it's about all of those that are connected to my life. God has always had a plan for my life and He has more than me in mind. So I had to get out of my way, and I had to stop being a victim to my fear.

Within the last 3-4 years, I began to realize how important my life is to the world. When I was just thinking of myself, it really didn't matter. I didn't try, and I didn't care. But when God opened my eyes to his promises, and allowed me to realize that I am a leader at work and at home, my life changed. I became hungry for learning more so that I could be more for others. I realized that I can't give what I don't possess. Somebody is waiting on my yes. Somebody needs to know that they too can break through. It is my duty and my responsibility to do something with what God has given me. He did not preserve and protect me through all of my foolishness for me to keep what I have learned to myself. He has commanded me to be bold and courageous enough to live my life out loud, regardless of what people say or who doesn't like it.

There are 3 ways that I began to see the power of my greatness, and I want to share them with you.

1. **Evaluate your circles**. You are the sum of the 3 people you hang around the most. Where are you spending your time? If it's not stimulating your growth, you should seek out a new circle.

2. **Get out of your comfort zone.** Trust me, the wall that you've built to protect yourself from hurt is only keeping you in a zone of mediocrity. Nothing great happens there. And your greatness won't be activated there. Go out and do the very thing God has called you to do. Will it be scary? Maybe. You won't know until you try.

3. **Do a life inventory.** Acknowledge where you are in life, and where you want to me. Create a blueprint of what it may take for you to get there. Put the right people in place to help you grow into that leader you were destined to be. Ask God to

129

show you the purpose driven people you need in areas of your life that you may be struggling in. It may be finances, romance, spiritual, physical or even your career. And be ready to move when God tells you to move.

What does greatness look like to you?

_____

_____

_____

Which of those 3 ways can you begin to implement in your life today?

_____

_____

_____

About the Author

A motivational speaker, consultant, author and facilitator, who specializes in navigating people through challenging and sometimes difficult situations in real life. NeeCee's approach is to assist others in regaining and maintaining their confidence, by creating a plan to stay on track, using her motto, "Keep it Simple." NeeCee's passion is to enrich, encourage and motivate others to realize that they do not have to settle for the hand that they have been dealt in life. Better and best are ALWAYS available. To find out more about NeeCee or to learn how she can help you move from good to great, follow her on social media via FB @NeeCee Speak or IG NeeCee Speaks Life or by email @neecespeaks@gmail.com

Dear fear, you tried it hold me down but unfortunately God has a better plan for me and each time you try to show up, I kick you down with my lovely boots and I keep it moving. I appreciate you for coming because you keep me on my toes and keep me pushing forward

Fabiola Giordani
www.fabiolagiordani.com

TRANSITION

BY MARIA BYRD

dear fear, you can't have my ...

Dear fear,

You Can't Have My Transition

◆————————————————————————◆

Dear Fear,

You have been in my life for such a long time, which is why I referenced you as dear. I want to tell you that playtime is over and I have allowed you to remain in my life for far too long. Because I have allowed you so much time, space and room to grow within my head, you have taken root. I must cut FEAR out of my life at the root because it has paralyzed me in my journey. Fear and Success cannot abide in me if I am a child of the most High God. 2 Tim 1:7 states, "For God gave us a spirit not of fear but of power and love and self-control." I have power and self-control over FEAR; it doesn't have control over me. I acknowledge that fear is a part of life, but it doesn't have to rule my life. I acknowledge that I catered to FEAR and have allowed it to consume my thoughts, which in turn halts me in my tracks from being all that I can be as an entrepreneur. I respect my mistakes in allowing fear to rule because I know it is only false evidence appearing real in my mind. I will not allow fear to manage my time and efforts, as I am walking by faith and not by sight. God said to "pray about it, not fear about it." I am declaring that I will pray for God's divine grace and mercy as I continue along this journey of a new discovery for my life. The Lord is walking with me because he put this business on my heart. I need to lean on him, as he has already equipped me with the knowledge and understanding of what I am supposed to do to help others along this path. I am saying goodbye to my fears and hello to confidence in knowing that God has allowed me to walk into the next chapter fully equipped to handle it. I will boldly walk into my destiny and claim the victory.

Signed
Maria Byrd,
NO longer FEARFUL of my FAILURES

I've dated fear for a long time, so long that it held a permanent role in my life. It started as the insecure girl in high school, transitioned with me as I joined the military, followed me as I progressed up the ranks, and followed me into retirement as a Chief Warrant Officer Four. There were five areas I noticed Fear ruled over me: fear of not being enough, fear of not knowing enough, fear of ending up like my parents (divorced), fear of not being capable enough to get my job done, and fear of failure. Fear has been there through it all, but in the end FEAR didn't win! I was beautiful enough (inside and out) to become a bride, and I was smart enough to enter as a Private First Class (PFC) and obtain SSG status before I crossed over to the Warrant Office Corp. I would go on to rise to the rank of Chief Warrant Officer Four (CW4). I obtained many other achievements throughout my military career and now I am smart enough, bright enough, strong enough, wise enough and capable enough to be the CEO of my own company. You see, FEAR was there all along pushing me to be the best I could possibly be, but I thought it was there to hold me back or just maybe I was the one holding myself back. Can you relate?

I want to ask you something. What is fear holding you back from at this very moment? I'll wait for you to answer in the area below.

_____

_____

_____

This little insecure girl from the first capitol of Georgia was leaving to find her place in the world. I joined the military at an early age, and fear placed doubt in my mind that I wasn't going to make it through basic training, that I would end up going home to my momma. I was so afraid of being so many miles from home, in an unfamiliar environment, new people, drill sergeants all around yelling at me for every little thing I did wrong. I soon realized that if I wanted to make it, I had to dig deep within and find that fortitude to study for exams, study my craft, learn to fire my M16 machine gun, learn to do physical training (exercise), but most importantly I had to learn to do it alone. You see there were no family members encouraging me to be strong. You can do it, hold your head up, take a breath, you were equipped for such a time as this, and never let them see you sweat. I had no one but myself and God. I motivated myself through the grace of GOD to take it one day at a time. I learned how to survive, I learned that I could do anything I set my mind to do if I believed in my God given talents. NO matter what challenges I have faced, GOD has been there every step of the way. There were times when things didn't work out. I realized I was not following my core beliefs nor was I following GOD's will.

Fast forward to me retiring from the military and FEAR rears his big fat head and places that doubt in me like nobody's business. I was so afraid to transition from the military. I couldn't remember what it was like to be a civilian. I was afraid that I wouldn't get it right. I was afraid that I wouldn't fit in. I was afraid that I wouldn't be a great wife or mom. I knew I wanted to start a business, but I allowed fear to tell me that I couldn't, that I didn't have what it took to be the CEO of my own life. I allowed fear to place me in the passenger seat of my own life. Fear told me that people would judge me. News flash! People judged Jesus Christ. Who am I to think people wouldn't judge me? I am so over fear at this point in my life because if I allow it to rule I will never live the life God has destined for me on the other side of my transition. I feel so liberated at this moment! Why, you may ask? Because I am finally telling my story, I am living my truth, I am not afraid to live on the other side of retirement. I can hold my head up high and thank God for the all those things that I went through and the things I have accomplished in my life. Before, I never looked at what I accomplished in my life and told God thank you for the ups and downs, highs and lows, the strange lands, familiar places and all those life lessons I've learned along the way. Now, I am so overcome with emotions of joy, laughter, pain, sorrow and most of all just plain ole gratefulness for God being who he is in my life.

What are some things you can celebrate today?

_____

_____

_____

You matter! If you are ready to create your healthy transition outside of military life head on over to www.militarywomenintransition.com and schedule a consultation. You deserve to live a happy, healthy life uncamouflaged. Join me, because I am excited to take this journey with you.

About the Author

Maria Byrd is a self-care expert whose work is uniquely designed to support women in transition out of service in the military and into healthy, well-adjusted lives as civilians. A 27-year veteran of the United States Army, Maria is dedicated to showing military women how to discover or return to their own identities once they hang up their uniforms and re-enter life after service. Discouraged by the lack of resources available to help her process the emotional adjustment of retiring from a life of service, Maria became determined to create her own. MilitaryWomeninTransition.com is a virtual support hub from women who are preparing to transition out of the military, and features *My Healing Box*, a self-care themed subscription service for military women. Learn more at militarywomenintranstion.com

JOURNEY

BY ETHEL J. DAVIS

dear fear, you can't have my ...hm

You Can't Have My Journey

"A woman with a voice is by definition a strong woman. However, the search to find that voice can be remarkably difficult." – Melinda Gates

We never know what life has in store for us. Growing up, we have a certain amount of confidence that our hopes and dreams will materialize. Plus, we live in a world that little girls are to be seen and not heard. When life throws the painful lemons laced with insecurities and fear, then you rely on your mind, body, and spirit to hear God's voice to resuscitate your life by playing "full out" with a fearless mindset.

Like Martin Luther King, I had a dream to become the first African-American "Barbara Walters" protégé as a successful journalist. As editor of my college newspaper, I believed in reporting information to make the reader feel empowered or bring awareness to sensitive subject matter that most would not approach. Not me, I felt a sense of obligation to separate the fiction from facts regardless of the consequences. I was living, breathing and fighting to be the vessel that delivers truth, hope, and peace within the community that I served. God had the plans, and I merely hung onto the goals.

Sometimes, God calls upon us to change lanes, proceed with caution but forge on to claim your blessings ordained by His grace and mercy. Regrettably, I did not get the memo regarding how to transition into a new career. I enjoyed working with numbers, assisting with personal and professional financial goals, and developing budgets, which led to my curiosity regarding the stock market.

This was the beginning of becoming a "Fearless" trailblazer due to stepping up and into a male-dominated industry, which was definitely "the good-old-boy" network. Every step was ordained by God because he knew the desires of my heart. The primary objective was to educate underserved communities with the principal of financial literacy and attributes of investing. Corporate America allowed me to start on the ground floor and God kept elevating me even when it did not make sense. I learned a variety of life lessons from legendary leaders from the financial community, faith-based women entrepreneurs (Women Who Mean Business) who were trailblazers paving the way for me until I could find my strength.

With fierce determination, the leap of faith guided me to step away from the corporate infrastructure and embraced the small business arena. I stayed true to succeeding as an African American woman, suffered through invisible glass ceilings, race and gender discrimination and a high level of harassment. Throughout the journey of my career, I sought mentors, femtors, and coaches to help me understand how to keep my authenticity and without diminishing my faith or passion.

This chapter strengthens my spiritual journey that comes from seeking God first without hesitation or fear. Unfortunately, I became acquainted with people who were "in charge" who never celebrated me, simply tolerated due to their insecurities and narcissistic demeanor. Like a bad marriage, I tried to play by their rules, but that did not agree with my soul or professional value proposition. This journey led to the birth of my company in 2012 – VZD Capital Management, a fee-based, Registered Investment Advisory firm located in Johnson County, Kansas. My courage grew into me becoming a respected financial advisor, a top minority business owner, recognized wealth manager, economic empowerment coach, and a results-driven businesswoman.

You never know what life has in store for you. My journey led me through setbacks that turned into setups, unexpected mess that became my message and tests that coauthored my testimonials.   Three themes that define my outlook on life since I turned fifty are: goals, plan and the ability to turn when you hit an unexpected detour. I have ridiculous work ethic, high goals and expectations, and I am no longer guided by someone else's rules – led by God's grace and mercy on this road to glory. I do not waste energy by holding grudges or hanging on to regrets. I count my blessings versus the stretch marks left by other people, editorials or negative descriptions regarding the episodes of my life. Currently, I use my experiences to help change myself and empower others to stand up for themselves without any excuses.

If I could have the opportunity to speak to my younger self, I would say, "Stay true to your goals, seeks God's plans, be flexible and adaptable to turn if you run into a roadblock." Let life happen and stop trying to be perfect by micromanaging everybody and everything. Midlife brings a calmness, you have settled into who you are and can just enjoy the ride. I stand available and open to follow God's lead to expand his Kingdom by being obedient to serving others – one client at a time.

Ethel J. Davis – is an American businesswoman who is the CEO and Portfolio Manager of VZD Capital Management, LLC. She is the first African-American female to own 100 percent of a Registered Investment Advisory firm in the Midwest and one of few within the United States. She celebrates 29 years of financial and investment experience by respected businesses – American Century, Fidelity Investments, Charles Schwab & Co., Inc and Paragon Capital Management, LLC. Ethel is a financial maven by leveraging her investment experience and circles in red life's lessons to understand each client's goals, objectives, time horizon and emotional state of mind. She makes it her mission to extract their stories, filter the information and then build a customized roadmap that fuels their legacy, dreams, honor their heritage and exceed their financial expectations

She is recognized for the following awards:

- Recognized by the Kansas City Business Magazine – 5 Star Wealth Manager

- Member of the prestigious Kansas City Business Journal Women Who Mean Business
- Ewomen Network Fearless Women
- The Kansas City Magazine Influential Women
- Member of Expert Network - an invitation-only service for distinguished professionals.
- Member of Heritage Who's Who in America
- Forbes Wealth Management 2017 and Beyond

VOICE

BY LAVOYDIS POWELL

dear fear, you can't have my ...

Dear fear,

You Can't Have My Voice

Dear Fear,

You. Can't. Have. My. Voice! I have been silent way too long. I hereby serve notice on you! You no longer reside in my mind, my heart, my space, my home, my present or my future. Buh-bye! Feel free to sit on the sideline and watch me exercise my faith over you! Yes, you are welcome to peek in the windows to see how I will flourish without you. But just a peek, because soon the curtains will be closing. Yes, it's Act 2. A whole new "scene" without you, FEAR! For far too long, I have allowed you to paralyze me and keep me from that which God has destined for me. No more! No more will I allow you to dictate my every move. No longer will I allow you to either whisper or bark out orders to me. No longer will I allow you to keep me from my purpose and my destiny.

You thought I was totally blind, didn't you? I see what you tried to do. I see how you slithered your way into my life like a snake, trying to wrap yourself around my hopes and dreams. You were trying to choke out my future.

I get it now. I see you for what you are, FEAR. You started your shenanigans when I was a little girl; timid, shy, and unsure of myself. Uh huh. Had me so busy focusing on what I thought were my shortcomings, that I didn't really see ME. The beautifully designed, blessed ME that God created. The gifted, talented (created for so much more) ME. You tried to make sure I didn't tap into my passions, my gifts and my talents. You wanted me to stay stuck, paralyzed and a disabled disaster. You wanted me to focus on you; (F)ailure (E)xpected (A)nd (R)eceived. You wanted me to expect to fail and receive whatever you said. No, not today or anymore! Step to the left fear. You tried to change me? Now I'm changing you! I am choosing to (F)ace (E)verything (A)nd (R)ejoice!

Oh fear, you are something else! I remember how you used to bully me as a little girl. Afraid to do this and afraid to do that. I remember the days when I did not want to raise my hand in class. You tried me every time, taking a seat in the desk beside me as if you were invited. I know you didn't like it when I fought back. I remember the days I used to hate to walk down the street. Sounds so simple, right? But I was tall for my age and lanky. No, not just lanky and thin; boney. Sometimes you would make me feel awful, like I was walking a tight rope when I walked down a street.

See, I didn't realize that I wasn't inadequate. I didn't realize that I was exactly the way I was supposed to be. I now see that you came around to stop me from walking. But I kept walking. Yes! I didn't know then that I was doing IT scared.

No, I'm not done! You want me to be done. You want me to be silent. But remember, I get it now. I have been silent for way too long! I look back at every stage of my life and realize how much you tried to muzzle me with your scare tactics. Fear, you didn't play fair. Now, I'm not playing fair!

You made me believe that people pleasing was the way to keep the peace. I was doing this for one and doing that for the other, just running. Tired and trying to please husbands, I was losing myself in the process. I never stopped to ask what I was afraid of. That question alone scared me and you knew that. You had me believing that walking on eggshells was the norm. Gingerly walking through days trying not to detonate another explosive situation. Yes fear, you had me owning problems, issues, and concerns that were not mine to own. You, fear, had me shouldering everyone else's baggage while I had heaps of my own on my back. Look fear, this chick has been in her shell long enough. She is breaking out! And the eggshells she used to tip toe through, she is praise dancing on!

I'm digging up roots, fear! Roots of your fear weeds that tried to poison and stifle this growing flower. The fear roots that had me afraid to speak up. The fear roots that told me like many others not to talk about pain, problems, and hurts. Your nasty roots had me worried about what people would think. Your nasty roots almost kept me from my destiny of encouraging and helping others.

No more! I have a voice! I'm singing like a songbird. You, fear, may have delayed me, but my destiny will not be denied.

Yes...it's Act 2...a whole new "scene" without you, FEAR!!! That's right! New Act. New scene. New chapter. Turning the page. I'm reclaiming my VOICE! I have spent way too much energy on you! As I grab hold to my possibilities, I now release what made things "seem" impossible. YOU!

Bye Fear!
Signed,
LaVoydis with a new Voice!

About the Author

LaVoydis Powell is an Emotional Strategist, Visionary, and the Host of The Gathering Experience, which offers a sisterhood of sharing and healing in a creative, fun-filled environment. LaVoydis has a passion for encouraging people, particularly women and young ladies, to live happy, healthy and whole lives by taking care of their spiritual, physical, and mental well-being. For more than 20 years, she has served as a mentor and life coach to numerous young ladies, empowering them to overcome life's challenges. Learn more at www.lavoydisspeaks.com

Dear fear, you have no place in my mind, my heart,

my spirit, and when you creep in I will shoot you

down the second you come in.

Natalie Gouche
www.nataliegouche.com

AUTHENTICITY

BY MICHELLE L. HAILEY

dear fear, you can't have my ...hui

Dear fear,

You Can't Have My Faith Or My Authenticity

Too often circumstance can dictate what we believe, how we act and how we identify ourselves. It is the story that we create, whether fact or fiction, that steers us in life. Throughout the journey, there are times when fear sits in the driver's seat and dictates the actions, behaviors, and decisions that we make. What causes this fear and where does it come from? What exactly are we afraid of? Fear manifests in many different ways for all people. In my case, there were times in my life when I feared being rejected, disliked, failing, and being exposed as a fraud. One of my earliest fears, of not being good enough, caused me to change direction in my life completely. I talked myself out of my first love, dance, because I did not think I was good enough. All I could envision was living in a closet in New York City, waiting tables and suffering through auditions where they would say, "Thanks, don't call us, we'll call you!" Not that there is anything wrong with living this life, but why suffer through all of that if I wasn't good enough in the first place? So, instead of facing the shadow of rejection and not being good enough, I decided to major in Fashion Merchandising and minor in Business instead of pursuing dance. This decision was a defining moment that marked my point of departure on the road to an inauthentic life, until ultimately the weight of wearing the many masks over the years took its toll. I became a shell of myself, someone that I did not even recognize. How did I get here? How do I find my way back? Faith in God and my spiritual foundation from childhood is what kept me through all of the challenging times. I knew that finding my way back would be to defeat fear with my faith by deepening my relationship with God. I had to stand up to fear's tests and do things afraid, confident that God had already made me victorious. During this process, it was necessary for me to be reflective and look over some of the pivotal phases in my life to see how I got to this place that could help lead me back to myself. Let's take a journey together that will explore various stops along the path of my life, giving you a small glimpse of the truth of who this South Jersey Girl is, and how she went from fear to faith and authenticity. There are three pivotal stops along this journey: The Genesis, The Awakening, and The Metamorphosis. But first, let's examine the girl…

What can you say about a girl who was born in Philadelphia, raised in a small town in Southern Jersey, went to college in Washington, DC, studied abroad in Paris, lived in New York City for almost 20 years, then landed in a remote village in Kenya before settling back in DC? Maybe you could say that she's a gypsy, a pilot, or maybe she's just an adventurer, an explorer on the journey we call life. When people ask me, "Who is this woman?" I tell them, "I'm a little French, African girl from South Jersey who loves God and family, enjoys Latin dance, and has a passion for empowering women and girls."

STOP #1 THE GENESIS

How it all began. This is a story about a childhood built on a foundation of faith, love, and acceptance, with a twist of a charmed life. I was always encouraged to be a free spirit and enjoy the things I loved, whether it was summertime at the Jersey Shore with the smell of funnel cake and cotton candy, playing on the beach with my two cousins, cheerleading in front of a rowdy crowd, roller skating, dancing, swimming or just hanging out with my family. These are some of my nostalgias of growing up in South Jersey. The funny thing is that I was such a tomboy. I had every color of high top Converse sneakers, and at the risk of dating myself, I also had an orange dump truck and GI Joe with the kung-fu grip. At the same time, you could find me playing with my Barbie and her dream home with Ken. I have always been eclectic and eccentric, and dared to be different. Whether it was dancing, playing baseball with the guys or flying to Jamaica on my swing, these things were some of the highlights of my young life.

One of my fondest memories, around age 5, was in my grandparents' backyard playing in the dirt with my overalls and high top sneakers on. I decided to get on my swing and fly. My grandfather, who I lovingly called "Pop-Pop," would push me in my swing. Pop-Pop would say, "Princess (that's what he called me), where are you going today?" I would reply, "I'm flying to Jamaica Pop-Pop. I'm flying to Jamaica." That was the beginning of my international travel. My passion for traveling and for other cultures was birthed that year and remains with me to this day. Life is just one big adventure. Where would I go next?

My parents, Judi and Michael (who I was named after) always supported freedom of speech, with respect of course, and encouraged my creativity and independence. In spite of my parents' divorce when I was very young (both remarried soon after), what would be a tragedy for some became a blessing that would lay a firm foundation of love and acceptance in my life. In years to come, our family became very blended; four parents, three sisters and two brothers, with me being the oldest. I still proudly hold the badge of honor of "FIRST BORN" to this day. However, in the process I appointed myself "Ms. Fix It," always working to keep the peace and make things okay for others. I would make sure everyone was getting along, loving each other and singing Kumbaya! I became the ultimate people pleaser to make sure that rejection would never be an issue. Little did I know this issue would come back up many years later.

STOP #2 THE AWAKENING

Although I visited many parts of the world in the GENESIS phase of my life, it wasn't until traveling to Kenya in 2007 that I experienced stop #2 on my journey - The Awakening. This excursion was a very cathartic and eye-opening experience. I fled to this developing, yet beautiful country to escape what was an extremely fearful and tragic time in my life. While I was there, I was also looking to work toward empowering women and girls as well as advance my passions and interests. Not only were there numerous opportunities to help these women, but I found that working with them helped *me* even more in the process. The people in Kenya were warm, welcoming and beautiful. They embraced me as if I was one of their own, and their sense of pride in themselves and their culture captivated me. The way they spoke so eloquently from the heart each time they addressed me was an "ah ha" moment. All of these years, I hid behind my fear and the masks of pretense, ego, and pride to keep people from seeing the insecurities that lie within. After three months of living in this fantastic place, I walked away from Kenya as a changed woman; more humble, more grateful, more open, more willing to begin facing my fears and living life "out loud." I emerged to release the hurts and pains of the past and began to embrace my eclectic uniqueness and my voice. Many people go through life on autopilot, in zombie mode, or living from the place of "same 'ole" whenever asked what's new.

To live a more faith-filled and authentic life, an awakening is necessary. This involves being true to your personality, spirit, values, beliefs, and character. Essentially, you must be true to yourself; not fake, but genuine and real. Somehow, I lost this along with the way. How often do we think about the core values in our lives and those things we did in our youth that gave us joy? Probably not much, if at all. I know, I can tell by your silent pause. Right now you're thinking, *"How can I experience my awakening?"* I'm glad you asked. Go back to the Genesis! Start by revisiting those things that grounded you and gave you joy in your youth, or explore something that you've always wanted to do, but were afraid to try; serve your local ministry, volunteer, salsa dance, rock climb, take a class, join a meetup group. One of the primary things that ground me is my faith in God. Although I have walked with Him since I was seven years old, I fell off the path many times along the way. But whenever I stopped and centered myself back to the core of who I am, it was my faith and relationship with God that brought me back to my authentic self. Even though I was a dancer growing up, the thought of becoming one as I approached my forties was an unfathomable idea. Thanks to my brother, Eric, encouraging me to take a step out of my comfort zone, I plunged into the deep and took up Latin dance. Taking this step was one of the best, most cathartic and impactful decisions I could have made at that time. Through nurturing this essential part of me, a creative side that had suffered years of neglect finally had an opportunity to emerge. Within a few months, I went from taking a weekly intermediate Salsa dance class to performing with the dance studio troop at the Tropicana Hotel in Atlantic City, NJ. Just the idea of performing as a professional, and *especially* at thirty-nine years old, was something that I had never imagined possible. Remember, the possibilities are endless, and it's NEVER too late. These are some of the things that I revisited to transition into the final stop on this phase of my journey, stop #3 - The Metamorphosis.

STOP #3 THE METAMORPHOSIS

Eight years ago, I entered this exhilarating, yet daunting phase of my life that I like to call "my metamorphosis." I was like a caterpillar in a cocoon changing into a butterfly. For me, it was relocating back to DC after almost twenty years and starting from scratch (no home, no job, and no "life" to speak of). Nevertheless, it was an opportunity to finally come into my own, do life on my terms, choose my destiny and ultimately discover how that looks and feels. Once I got my footing in my new DC life, I decided to incorporate the truths that are at my core into my everyday life; Love God, Love Family, Love People. I forced myself to step out of the box, out of my comfort zone and launch out into the deep. Some of the other intentional choices that I made were to connect with a local church, find fun places to salsa dance whenever I got the chance and joined Toastmasters to help my career. Participating in each of these activities took me outside of my comfort zone in one way or another. Nonetheless, I wanted to establish spiritual relationships, nurture my creative and artistic culture, and hone my professional skills, all while becoming more empowered with each accomplishment, equipping myself to empower others.

Overall, my life has been an incredible journey with a bit of fear entwined throughout. In the latter part of my genesis state, I lost myself, forever showing up as what I wanted the world to see. Always searching for perfect, always presenting perfect, always striving for perfect. I attracted hurt. Instead of facing my fears head on, I continued wearing the masks, resulting in more years of fear that people would find out my secret. Wearing the mask of inauthenticity is exhausting and eats away at your spirit, self-esteem, and confidence everyday. I woke up one day feeling like a shadow of the person I once was, which led me to my awakening. It was that moment when I was on the floor asking God to either fix my broken marriage or

163

release me, that I knew my life had to change. In relatively short order, the answer came through much chaos and turmoil that flung the door of opportunity wide open. I fled, never looking back. My life depended on it. My purpose depended on it. My destiny depended on it. I was lost, broken and exhausted, trying to keep the masks up and not wanting anyone to see the truth of what was hiding behind them.

Fear convinced me that if I left, my life would be over. The truth is, my life didn't start until I left that girl who had become a shell of the God fearing, family oriented, fun, talented, adventurous, vivacious person she once was. One of the most hurtful things about being in that situation was that it was something that I chose and allowed, and the onus for that part was on me. As I transitioned from that place, I entered into this season of awakening; I like to say I was saved by Esther. Although I knew that God had already orchestrated the plan for my future, I was saved by His grace through this extraordinary woman of God. After just meeting me a few hours before through a very good friend, she immediately saw my brokenness and pain. She opened up her heart and said, "You need to come home with me." My first thought was, *To Africa?* But what did I have to lose? I accepted her invitation and stepped out on faith, leaving behind all of the comforts of home (family, friends, job, etc.) to travel to the foreign, yet familiar land of Kenya Africa. My sister, friend, and mentor, Dr. Esther Keino, welcomed me and my healing began. During the three months I was there, I felt my heart beat again. It beat again for me, for my faith, my family and my purpose. Through the gripping clutch of the purging process, God was reviving me and giving me another chance at living the abundant, faith-filled, authentic and divinely whole life He has for me.

Fear has a way of showing up when you least expect it, especially at the most inopportune moments. Whether it comes in the form of people pleasing to avoid rejection, talking yourself out of doing something that you love for fear that you're not good enough, or putting on the masks fearing that everyone will see your flaws and insecurities. Despite whatever fears you may face, my challenge to you is to stand up to your fears and do it for yourself, even if you are afraid. Who do you want to be? How will you show up in *your* life? How do you want to be remembered? What will be the legacy you leave to the world, whether that world is in the lives of people you touch, your home, church, community, or any other arena where you dwell. In the meantime, just remember, **#1 THE GENESIS, #2 THE AWAKENING AND #3 THE TRANSFORMATION.**

It's never too late to discover the real you. While much of this work you will have to do for yourself, it is crucial to know that you cannot go on this journey alone. We are all at various stages along our paths, and part of facing your fear is not being afraid to seek help and support from others. It may only take one, even if that one merely holds your hand to guide you to the next step. Let me just say that had it not been for the fantastic people in my life, there is no way I would have been able to survive the journey and emerge in such a beautiful sense. I thank them, thank God for them, and am genuinely grateful for their love and support throughout the journey. Along my path, I have doubted myself, God and whether I would ever see the other side of fear. This journey has given me many rich opportunities to finally walk firmly in my faith in God, trusting and believing in Him and myself, and confidently knowing the truth; that I am enough, I am valuable, I am significant, I am faith-filled, and I am authentic! Being true to yourself and what you believe is the key to living life "out loud." Come, join me on this incredible, cathartic journey to faith and an authentic you. Because as long as we are alive and the journey continues, there is liberty!

When was a time that you did not feel Authentic?

_____

_____

_____

What (1) step are you willing to take in the next 30 days to get in touch with your Authentic self?

_____

_____

Michelle L. Hailey is a business professional who has used her global experience and talents to cultivate her areas of expertise in program management, training and development, mentoring, strategic planning, communications and consulting. She has a passion for educating, impacting, empowering and inspiring the lives of others to excel within the global community. Whether speaking, training, consulting, mentoring or embarking on new initiatives, one of Michelle's goals is to combine her background, passion for empowering others, global experience, with her knowledge of business, the arts, entertainment and social entrepreneurship to promote success in her future endeavors. As a woman of faith, she believes in the concept of teaching a person how to fish so they can live for a lifetime versus giving them a fish only to eat for a day. Each one, reach one and teach one.

dear fear, let go of my ...

BOOTSTRAPS

BY LORENDA CHISOLM

Dear fear,

Let Go of My Bootstraps

◆————————————————————————◆

"Table for one, please." Yes, it was awkward at first. You see, like many women, I dreamed of marriage, living in a nice house, having children, and landing a dream job (career). And that is exactly what I had accomplished. Not necessarily in that particular order, but I felt for the most part that I had done well. As a matter of fact, I had obtained almost every goal that I set. I had created vision boards, lists of short and long-term goals, worked hard, and tried to position myself in spaces and places that would help me elevate, all in an effort to support my family. I did the work! So why was I now, sitting at a table for one?

Twenty years ago, I met my ex-husband. I was a senior in college and he was 14 years my senior (Sign #1). He was already divorced and had a baby by a woman other than his ex-wife when I met him. As I approached graduation, I brought up the possibility of us moving in together. He felt I wasn't ready, so I began to search for an apartment of my own. I ended up landing a job just before graduation and he remarkably ended up agreeing that we should move in together (Sign #2). I initially felt like he changed his mind because it would be better financially for him, but I quickly got that out my head and figured it was because we were planning to be together. Two years later we were engaged, and I was pregnant soon after. Because his son lived with us, we knew it was time to move out of our 2-bedroom apartment, so we purchased our first home. Two years later we were married. But wait, let me not skirt over the fact that while we went to handle the behind-the-scenes paperwork in preparation for marriage, I learned he was still carrying his ex-wife on his insurance (Sign #3). He had also been living and working under his stepfather's last name, which was not his legal last name (Sign # 4). How was this even possible? Was this not important to share? And, who the hell's last name would I be taking? But it didn't matter. I was happy. I felt we were already too invested. I loved him and we already had a family.

We took cross-country road trips, admired each other, loved on each other (even in some interesting places), hosted get-togethers with family and friends, and made each other laugh. It was to the point that as a baby, our daughter referred to both of us as 'mommy-daddy'. There was no differentiation. We had such a love and respect for each other that even the signs couldn't deter me – or so I thought. What I didn't realize, was that it was all a charade; the love, the respect, the image, the whole persona was a lie. As time went on, I learned that the man I trusted to protect and lead couldn't manage finances, leaving me to dig us out of debt time and time again (Sign #5). In addition, he would have multiple affairs. There were four that I found out about, so you know there was a very strong possibility there were more (Signs #6-10). I began to feel resentful. I knew that I could no longer pretend the signs were not there. Something had to give...and so it did.

Four years ago my divorce was finalized. My now ex-husband, had told me over the phone that we needed to talk when I got home from work. That evening, we went for a walk around the corner, and that's when he told me he wanted a divorce. He tried to package his words up with a pretty bow, but I wasn't buying it. As a matter of fact, after a short while, I couldn't hear much of anything he was saying to me because on the inside I was furious, but I was trying to play cool because we were out in public. In fact, I'm sure that was his intent. All I could think to myself was, *Did this man really just 'walk me' to tell me he wanted out?* I knew it had to involve another woman even though he was trying to sound diplomatic. It was like I literally tuned him out and started having a conversation in my head about my next move. The charade was that he was a faithful and doting husband, that he had his stuff together (finances), and he was honest. When in fact, he couldn't remain faithful, he continuously mismanaged funds, and he was manipulative. The truth is, it did involve another woman.

That night, as *we* lay in bed, I replayed our conversation. I started having flashbacks of everything we had been through over the years, including the signs that I didn't pay much attention to in the beginning. It was at that very moment that fear began to creep in like a thief in the night. As the silent tears rolled down my face, I realized I was afraid and alone in bed with a stranger. I was now overcome with fear of being by myself, living and growing old alone. I feared being a single parent and was unsure how to do it alone. I feared other people's perceptions of me as a single parent. I feared managing my home alone. I feared no one would want a woman with a child. I feared that I had failed my daughter and that she would see me as a failure. I feared that I had failed myself. I was so overwhelmed with fear that self-doubt had knocked at the door. I questioned if I was ever enough, and if he was either. As the days went by, I tried to process what was going on in my life. Each time I thought about it, I became overwhelmed with emotions. I was hurt, sad, disappointed, frustrated, scared, angry, resentful, nervous, unforgiving, bitter, and numb. Before I knew it, I realized I was functionally depressed. I was experiencing grief. Yet, I still had to wake up each morning, go to work during the day, attend classes in the evenings, and still be a mother. I had actually considered not continuing in my doctoral program because I was unsure of myself and how I was going to navigate this process under these circumstances. I vividly recall having a moment in my advisor's office and being told that I could "take time off" if I needed to. Instead of walking away, I was able to bring my daughter to class with me. There were some nights we ate dinner in the student union and had homework/study time in the student lounge or the school library. All I can say is, I'm so glad I didn't quit. Not only would I have never forgiven myself, but I would have given *him* more credit than he deserved.

This man had caused me to internalize *his* feelings, question myself, feel like I was to blame for everything; and I actually believed I was for a short while. I had actually relinquished my emotional control to someone who no longer deserved me, who no longer wanted me, and who no longer loved or valued me. And once I realized this, the rational part of me decided it was time to seek counseling - so I did, and it was 'alright'. When he decided to move out, all I could do was look him in the eyes and tell him that once he left he could never come back. I can still see the look in his eyes when those words flowed from my lips. After three months of him being gone 'sewing his royal oats', I served him with divorce papers. I realized there was absolutely no way I was going to sit around, still married, and wait on him while he lay up with another woman. This was the beginning of my breakthrough.

My divorce took a year. During this time, I felt as though each day I got closer and closer to regaining my control and independence. I grew stronger in my faith, stronger in my vision, stronger in love with myself, stronger in my identity and sense of self, and stronger in my role as a mother. I wanted to make sure I didn't project my emotions onto her, while letting her know that she would be protected and we would be 'ok' no matter what. There is so much I can't fit into this story, but let me just say that as a result of my marriage and the bitter ending, I harbor physical scars that I must carry for the rest of my life. However, I'm more than thankful I'm not emotionally scarred. I remain faithful in what God has in store for me and in how He continues to provide for me. I know this lesson almost broke me, but in all things I give thanks. It has taught me to trust my instincts and not to settle, how to rely on my gifts and talents to pull me through tough times, to identify the feelings attributed to the fear and how to protect myself from going to that space again.

There is a fundamental difference between struggling and facing a challenge. Struggles are difficult encounters we are faced with when we are dissatisfied with some part of our life, while a challenge is an undertaking that leads to growth and lessons learned. How you approach what life throws at you will determine if you find yourself facing a challenge or in the midst of a struggle. You too, may face a challenge that leads you to adjust your path while aspiring to maintain your vision. Everyday I found a message that served as a gentle reminder of hope and faith during one of the most challenging times in my life. I filled my mirror with sticky notes containing motivational messages. Instead of holding me back, fear began to motivate me to keep moving onward and upward. If I had quit school, I would only resent myself for allowing a temporary situation to negatively impact a life-long goal.

In refocusing on my spiritual self, I had to really remember who I was and whose I was. I could often hear my late maternal grandmother reminding me of whose blood runs through my veins, relying on the knowledge that I come from a legacy and lineage of strong, devoted, and loving women and secure in the fact that I have a solid example of men in my life that I love and admire. I had to pick myself up by the bootstraps, lace them up nice and tight, and continue my stride--one foot in front of the other. Since then, I have traveled to many parts of the world, earned promotions in a career I love, grown closer to my daughter, and found ways to maintain peace from within. Through each experience, I learned to live in the moment and trust what lies ahead of me –

both known and unknown, and rely on my own inner compass (instincts) as my guide.

Hindsight is always 20-20. But come on, how many of us in retrospect say to ourselves, "I shoulda, coulda, woulda?" You see, it's ok to experience feelings of fear, hurt, guilt, anger, self-doubt, and even helplessness to some degree. It's absolutely normal. Whatever it is that has allowed fear to grab hold of you, remember those feelings you are experiencing, acknowledge them, and move. I say all this to say, you may find yourself stuck in fear - just don't become paralyzed. KEEP IT MOVING! Don't let fear grab a hold of your bootstraps. You must get to a point where fear motivates you to just get up and put those boots on. I don't care if they are flat or 6-inches high. Lace them up, pull tight, and double knot them if you have to. Just make sure you move with a purpose and always in a positive direction, high-stepping with one foot directly in front of the other.

I am learning to trust, even in the process of writing this chapter and exposing my vulnerability. I can't tell you how many people have told me I came through this storm like a champ or that no one would have never known all that I was going through by the way I handled myself on the outside. But because I love me, I can love you enough to reach back by sharing my story. Don't be afraid to love again, especially yourself. *"Table for one, please."*

When did you realize fear had you by the bootstraps and how did you demonstrate resiliency when facing fear?

_____

_____

_____

How does your sense of self-worth play into how you respond to fear?

_____

_____

_____

About the Author

Lorenda Chisolm is the mother of a beautiful daughter, Aziza and a central office school administrator. Prior to her current position, she served as a school counselor, assistant principal and principal. She earned a Bachelor's degree in psychology, a Master's in Counseling and Human Services, and a second Master's in Educational Leadership and Supervision, all from Canisius College in

Buffalo, NY. Most recently, she earned a Doctor of Education in Educational Administration from the University of Buffalo's Graduate School of Education. In addition, Lorenda is first author on a book chapter accepted in *Leadership, Culture and School Success in High-Need Schools.* Lorenda has received numerous recognitions for her hard work and dedication to the field of education. Her recognitions include Buffalo Business First 2015 '40 Under 40' honoree and the 2015 Women "Touching the World" Award in honor of National Women's History Month. She was also named as a 2014-2016 Jackson Scholar through the University Council for Educational Administration (UCEA).

POSITION

BY TYRA D. DYSON

dear fear, you can't have my ...

Dear fear,

You Can't Have My Position

"When you own your position, no one can take your place." ~
Tyra Dyson

⬦————————————————————⬦

"That's it, we're out of here!" That's what my mom said when she found out that the Klu Klux Klan was holding meetings just a few miles from where we lived, in my Dad's hometown of Louisville, KY in the late 70's. That was the last straw for the city girl from Washington, DC (also known as "Chocolate City" because of the large African American population).

I was born and raised mostly in Washington, DC, but when I was around 5 my mom moved us out of DC to live with my dad. During the few years we lived with my dad, I had experienced so many things that would shape the way I looked at life and the person I became. I had experienced my first road-trip, train ride, and flight. I lived in a house with two parents in a healthy relationship, I had my own room and a separate playroom full of toys, and we ate out at Red Lobster and Ponderosa Steak house without a special occasion! The schools I attended and the neighborhoods I lived in were a diverse mix of people from different racial and socioeconomic backgrounds. I had character building experiences and developed some culture, which gave me different perspectives than most of my peers at that time. We moved back to DC when I was 9, without my dad. And just like that, that part of my journey was over, but those experiences stayed with me forever. Little did I know a new journey was about to begin and life was about to get real.

The next few years of my life would be very different from what I had become used to and I would soon learn that the life I had experienced and thought was normal, was *not* so normal. Shortly after our return to DC, my mother became pregnant with my brother. I was no longer an only child and my mom was a single parent. She was unemployed with no money, and we stayed with relatives and in shelters until we finally got our own place. I attended at least seven elementary schools before the 6th grade, and I felt pressured to fit in with the new crowd and culture of every school I attended. I was constantly teased about "talking white," although I had no clue what talking white was. Over the next few years, we struggled. We were on welfare and food stamps. I remember not having enough to eat, utilities being cut off, and shopping at the thrift store. Things were difficult for us, and I was exposed to things a child shouldn't be and as a result some terrible things happened to me that no one should have to experience, especially a child. This is where I believe my fears and insecurities were born. All of this was a culture shock for me and for the first time, I realized what it was like to be poor and I didn't like it. I longed for the life I had before with my dad and I spent a lot of my life trying to get that back.

"Don't underestimate the impact your early childhood experiences will have over your life."

Growing up during the 80's was hard, it was one of the toughest economic eras in our country and "Reaganomics" were in full effect. The national debt nearly tripled, crack was introduced into poor black communities, and we learned AIDS was not only a white gay man disease; "Breaking News! *Magic Johnson has HIV!"* The economy was so bad, people were turning to crack, either as a dealer to get paid or a user to cope with being poor (*"Desperate people do desperate things"*). Crime was at an all-time high and DC was the murder capital of the world. These were scary times, people were struggling and depressed. I hated being poor and the position it put you in, because I watched what it did to my mom as she struggled to raise two kids on her own. She was the only one of her three sisters that never married, so no alimony or child support for her. She was alone, and after a few bad situations and a failed relationship, life had taken its toll on her. She turned to drugs to cope, which led to a twenty-year drug addiction and left her with a permanent health condition (consequence).

"Desperate people do desperate things".

It was hard for me to watch my mom suffer with addiction because she was the most courageous and confident woman I had ever known, and that experience made me fearful of what my own future would be like. I was determined not to put myself in a "position" to have that become my reality. **"My biggest fear was that I would end up poor, struggling, and alone."**

Growing up I often escaped my reality to protect and keep my dreams alive. I would ride the bus for two hours just to go to the movies in an affluent neighborhood. The air seemed fresher, sidewalks cleaner, and the people didn't seem to have a care in the world. I wanted that life. I would sit, have ice cream and people watch while I day dreamed. You see, I was giving myself a vision outside of my reality and preparing myself to be in position to experience a better life.

It's very hard to envision for yourself what you can't see. That's why experience and exposure is EVERYTHING! Don't be afraid to create your own vision and experiences.

When I was finally old enough to get a job, and make my own money I felt so empowered. I thought making money would put me in a position for better. For the first time, I believed I had control over my life and my future. I had very good grades in school, but I never thought I could afford college so I didn't bother to apply (BIG MISTAKE). After high school, I was excited to start my new life and escape my past. I was also terrified of becoming an adult, and life had a few surprises of its own. Shortly after I started working, my mom and I had an argument and she put me out of the house. I was 18. I slept on my aunt's couch for a few months until I could rent my first apartment. I was finally on my own, making money, and things were looking good. I was in position to be somebody, and then the curve ball! I became pregnant and quit my job, because of my own selfish insecurities aka fear. I was 19 years young and alone. I didn't have to quit but fear of embarrassment convinced me I had to. Once again, I was feeling stuck. It seemed as soon as I would take two steps forward, I would be set ten steps back! Do you know what it feels like to be in this position? It sucks! *Note to Self:*

1. *Never make any decisions out of fear and desperation.*

2. *Don't be anxious, take your time to think things through, exercise patience and wait for the right answer.*

3. *Have a good support system.*

Say to those who have an anxious heart, "Be strong; fear not! Behold, your God will come with vengeance, with the recompense of God. He will come and save you." ~**Isaiah 35:4**

Right after my daughter was born, I was holding her one day and I just broke out crying. I realized that I was responsible for another person's life and future, and I hadn't figured out my own yet. I was scared to death! I was sitting there thinking, *Oh Lord what have I done, I don't know what I'm doing.* I started having these fears, doubts, and worries about failing as a parent. My newest fear was repeating the same generational cycle of my upbringing. You see, I became pregnant at the exact same age my mother was with me, and like her, I had no job or husband and I would be raising my child as a single parent. All I could think was *how did I end up in this position?* All the fears of my childhood came rushing down on me and I was so afraid for my daughter's future. But ironically, my daughter had also given me so much hope and promise for my own future. Life was giving me a clean slate to create something great in her that I could be proud of. I made the decision to dedicate my life to making sure that her life would be much better than mine. I looked Fear in the face and said, "Nope, not my baby. You can't have her future or mine, so get ready for a fight!"

To see my dreams realized, I knew I needed another job (or so I thought). I had very few professional influences growing up and I found it difficult to find jobs where I fit in and felt valued, or where I didn't have to deal with office politics. Times got tough and between jobs I found myself on welfare and food stamps, and I hated it. I could never understand how people got used to being a slave to a system that is clearly set up to keep you on it. Working in corporate America was a challenge because it exposed so many of my fears and insecurities. Fear had me afraid to apply for jobs that required a college degree, and when I got the courage to apply for higher positions, fear told me I wasn't ready and would fail. *Fear of success is real.* I pressed my way through it anyway because in my mind I had nothing to lose. Every corporate job I've ever had required a college degree, and I got them all! #Faith. Corporate America sometimes felt like modern day slavery. Most employees were overworked, underpaid, and undervalued. I was always being reprimanded for my honesty after being "asked" my opinion. I found myself constantly defending my confidence and point of view, being *branded* argumentative, controversial, and my favorite "combative". I had to endure supervisors and colleagues being "indirectly" racist and blatantly disrespectful. Once, I even put my child's life at risk trying to punch a clock! One morning I was running late for work and took a taxi. I had the taxi take me to work first and then gave them the address to drop my 3-year-old daughter off at my mother's house. (Don't judge me! Okay...maybe judge me.) *What the heck was I thinking?* I was more fearful of losing my job than losing my child. (*Desperate people, do desperate things.*) God protected my child that day, I may have never seen her again. Every time I think about it still makes me want to cry. It's heartbreaking to know that I let someone invoke that kind of fear in me to put my child in such a dangerous position. And to top it off, I was still fired!

Note to self: You will never be able to truly settle down and accept something that is not meant for you. You will always be uncomfortable in that environment, so in the end, it doesn't pay to compromise your integrity or who you are for anyone. You only get one life, so do what you love and be happy.

I was unhappy, miserable really, because I was tired of sacrificing my integrity for a paycheck. Now here I am again, back in the same position of lack and defeat having to start over again. My relationship started to suffer, but I ignored it. I wanted to make sure that my daughter knew what it was like to live with both of her parents. I didn't want to be the baby mama and I didn't want the drama; I know how that story ends. I was determined to keep me and her dad together by any means necessary, so my daughter could have a good life and stable home environment. I allowed the fear of being alone control me and I tolerated a lot of things that compromised my self-respect & self-worth (again), things that really didn't set a good example for my daughter. My inconsistent employment and lack of financial stability, put me in a very vulnerable position and made me a dependent! I settled to maintain the lifestyle I had created for my daughter and myself even though I wasn't happy #nofaith. I learned a lot of HARD lessons over 25+ years, and often ask myself was it worth it. When I think about my daughter's life growing up and the adult she has become, I say yes. However, I wish I was in a better position to have done things differently, but with the same end result. It's funny how you can demand respect and be intolerable of behaviors in certain areas of your life, but not in others. Things that make you go hmmmm.

Note to self: LOVE YOURSELF FIRST! Never compromise and never settle. You must believe that you deserve the very best there is to offer in Love and in Life you must choose faith over fear.

I had become so depressed about my relationship and position in life that I developed a shopping addiction to cope. No drugs or alcohol for me, but an addiction just the same. It caused me to behave recklessly and make some irresponsible decisions that almost cost me my freedom and my future (*Desperate people, do desperate things*). My daughter was only ten years old at the time, and I remember getting on my knees and praying to God that if he got me out of this situation I would NEVER put myself in this type of position again. I was so afraid of never seeing my daughter again and worried what her future would look like if the full consequences of my actions were realized. Needless to say, my God never FAILS! From that point forward, I vowed to spend my life trying to be better and do better; and to help others do the same. Oh, there was an expensive consequence to pay, one that left a scar on my character, but good thing I get to create my own brand. You'll catch that later.

Note to self: God put you on this earth to do great things, and he gave you all the tools you need to succeed, Never, let anything or anyone jeopardize your position in life.

That experience changed my life forever, the fear of having my freedom taken away made me fight harder to keep it. My corporate experiences stirred my motivation for entrepreneurship, but this confirmed my purpose. I needed to be in control of my destiny and own my happiness. In the beginning, I had more failures than wins, and more financial losses than profits; but I was determined not to give up. Not until I joined forces with my daughter to start P2P Branded did I experience real success and freedom in business. Our company helps entrepreneurs build brands that matter. *"No one can represent your brand better than you"*. Building this legacy with my daughter has made me proud of the name I once was ashamed #TeamDyson. Fear would no longer make me desperate, dictate my future, or affect my position in life.

"Fear You Can't Have My POSITION to be GREAT!

Purpose, **O**pportunity, **S**uccess, **I**ntegrity, **T**ransformation, **I**mpact, **O**verflow, **N**ame (*Brand*)

About the Author

Tyra Dyson, CMP is the Co-Founder and one-half of the Mother & Daughter duo that is P2P Branded. She serves as the Director of Live Events & Personal Brand Strategist within her company. A serial entrepreneur Tyra found ways to link her life's passions with her personal gifts and started several businesses. Growing up she realized there was a lack of professional influence, but still envisioned herself as a successful business owner one day. She has worked hard to be the positive example for others she never had. Her skills for planning & organizing events lead her to a successful career in meeting & event planning and earning her Certified Meeting Professional (CMP) designation. Tyra strongly believes that how you represent yourself has a direct impact on your success and the opportunities that you receive. Tyra is a speaker & trainer dedicated to showing people how to use their gifts to start and grow a business doing what they love. Tyra's motto in life is to use your brand to RISE *(Represent In Style & Excellence)*. Learn more about Tyra at www.p2pbranded.com

Fear will not take my courage; Courage to stand, courage to just be me and to learn to walk in my destiny. I love ME!!

-Evelyn Nelson-

PAST

BY SHALON BARNETT

dear fear, you can't have my

...

Dear fear,

You Can't Have My Past

◆————————————————————————————————◆

Dear Fear,

For the past 10 years, I have allowed you to control my life. I have been afraid to travel, afraid to be around people and afraid to speak in front of people. I have been so busy starting projects that I never finished most of them because of you. I have been walking around pretending to be happy and giving hope to everyone else's dream but my own. I have been shopping every week trying to fill a void. I thought getting married, having a child, buying the house of my dreams, starting a business and being financially secure would fulfil me, but I still feel empty. Don't you have enough friends? Why are you constantly following me? I'm tired of fighting you. It's exhausting. I'm ready to take my power back. I won't allow you to convince me to hold onto things I should have let go of a long time ago. I'm done with you. Sorry, not sorry. Signed, Shalon

Ten years ago, my life was turned completely upside down when I came face to face with fear. It started one morning in late March, as I was walking my 9-year-old son to school. As I made it to the sidewalk in front of the house, I saw three unmarked police cars approach us. Immediately, I ran back into the house, leaving the front door open. The officers proceeded to come inside and spoke 10 words that forever changed the course of my life.

"WE HAVE A WARRANT FOR YOUR ARREST FOR MEDICAID FRAUD."

I knelt down and told my son to walk to school and mommy would see him later.

At first, I thought my arrest was a matter of going to jail, getting a bail amount and bonding out with no one knowing but me and God. I had been to jail quite a few times before, so I knew the routine. At least I thought I knew the routine. Before, I would be given a bail amount and would bond out in the same day. This was a totally different experience. As I sat in an open waiting area of the jail, I decided to call my friend to see what was taking so long. When my friend realized it was me, she said, "Shalon, sit down." In this moment I realized two things. One, apparently my friend had never been to jail because there is nowhere to sit while you are on the phone; and two, that she didn't have good news to deliver. "You were on the news."

My heart sunk to my feet, and I went numb. At that moment, fear started speaking to me. *You are never going to amount to anything. You are going to turn out just like your uncle. Didn't I tell you that you could never outrun who you are destined to be? A fraud.* As long as I could remember, my uncle was a fraud. He robbed places and people all the time. By the time I was eight, my uncle was murdered by the police after robbing a restaurant. Fear stayed with me, reminding me of where I was from; a small town where it only took one person to see or hear about me on the news in order to make me the "talk of the town." When I was finally released from jail later that day, I had more than 100 missed calls on my phone. I was so embarrassed that I couldn't respond.

Have you ever feared what would happen if you lost it all? That was me. In a short period of time, my life crumbled. Bit by bit, I lost nearly everything I had worked hard for. I lost the ability to run my business and make money. Fear began speaking again. *How are you going to support your son? He has never been able to depend on his father, and now he won't be able to depend on you. I guess you will have to move back to that small town and be the girl everyone said you would be...nothing.*

Before my arrest, I had built my business to the point that I was profiting $16,000 - $20,000 per month. But, I wasted most of the money I made by helping everybody around me and living how I wanted. I gave a lot of money away. What I didn't give away, I shopped away by buying whatever I wanted. I also bought my son anything he wanted, or I wanted him to have because I felt it made up for the times I wasn't with him due to work. Sadly, I hadn't saved any money. And after my arrest, I wasn't able to save because there was nothing to save. The irony.

People came and offered support, but it was time to give the support they vanished. Fear entered again and said, *I told you the only reason people were around you was because you had something to give; now that you are broke, they are gone. I told you so. I told you so.* I felt all by myself, alone and hopeless. I did not see a way out of the situation and just wanted to give up on life. Fear started talking yet again. *There is no way you are coming out of this; you should just end your life. All hope is gone, and no one will miss you.* Fear nearly won.

I remember choosing the day I would end my life. I was home alone and I cried the whole day. As I sat on the kitchen floor sobbing, ready to end it all, I closed my eyes and saw small snapshots of me standing in front of people and speaking. In that moment, I felt God's grace. He was giving me a preview of my life if I put my faith in him. That was my I Corinthians 10:13 moment, because it was my way of escaping suicidal thoughts. I Corinthians 10:13 says, *"No temptation has overtaken you except such as is common to man; but God is faithful, who will not allow you to be tempted beyond what you are able, but with the temptation will also make the way of escape, that you may be able to bear it"* (New King James version).

In that moment, I started having different thoughts. I thought about my son and how it would be extremely hard for him to make it in the world without me. I remembered my precious young boy who was so perfect in all his ways. I loved him more than life and death; he became my hope to get off the floor and figure out a plan. So, I had to let go of the pity party and suck it up. Fear had to take the backseat.

I took a plea bargain for my pending case and was offered five years of probation and restitution payments of the $3,000; I allegedly overbilled for this amount. I decided to let my son move in with my grandfather and aunt until I could get a job and find a stable place to live. This process took a year. I found a job, had a little car and signed a lease to my own apartment for us. As we settled into our new home, everything seemed to be going well, until Sunday, April 20, 2008. My son and I were riding to church, when I passed a police car that pulled out behind me. I did not pay the car any mind until the lights turned on and the officer motioned for me to pull over. I pulled over, then gave the officer my license and registration. He came back to the car and said, "Can you please step out of the car?" Anyone who has ever been pulled over knows those are the scariest words you ever want to hear, because behind those words are the worst words to hear. "You are under arrest for ......you have the right to remain silent; anything you say can and will be used against you in a court of law; you have the right to an attorney. If you cannot afford one, one will be appointed to you in a court of law. Do you understand these rights I have read to you?"

As I heard those all too familiar words, fear showed up again. *I told you that you are a failure, trying to move into this fancy neighborhood. You will never live the way you once lived. Ha Ha Ha!"* I already knew I was going to jail because part of my probation agreement was no contact with the police. This time it was for expired driving documents. (Can I please get a break?!) Fear kept talking to me. *This is the second time your son saw you get arrested. You should have taken your life. You mean him no good. You are going to be in and out of jail the rest of your life. You already have eight mugshots. What example are you showing your son? He has an absent father, and now you are leaving him with someone else again.* I had nothing to fight fear this time; I knew I would be in jail a little while. I assumed that it would take at least three days until I would be able to be seen by the judge. So, instead of holding my head low, I decided to start a 3 day journey to free my mind while I was waiting to be freed.

Day 1- I talked to everyone, trying to see the normal steps for a 1st time offender violating probation.

Day 2- I read books trying to rush the time, knowing I only had a few days before getting out and resuming my life. This time, I was arrested for driving with a suspended license. I had experience with this kind of case.

Day 3- I waited and wondered why I had not been set a court time to see the judge.

Day 7- (Wait, day 7?) I transferred to another jail.

Day 8 – I met new inmates and asked more questions on how long the process would take and when I would get a court date.

Day 10 – I waited on my first visit with my son. I did not want him to see me in jail, but I missed him. The visit did not happen because I was transferred to another jail in another county.

Day 11- The 3 day freedom journey turned into a personal detox that changed my life forever. I started to question myself. *How did I get here? What did I need to do not to return? How could I change my life?*

Day 12- I started deep self-evaluation by talking to God and coming up with a plan to never get myself in this situation again. I started going to every bible study offered in jail, trying to understand why I was in jail so long. Transformation started in my life after I made up my mind to make some changes in my current situation.

Day 19- I finally had a court date; adjudication was withheld, and my probation was reinstated. I was informed that I would be released that day!

Though I was excited, fear surfaced again. *Where are you going to live? You will have to send your son back with your family. Why do you try so hard? You will never be anything.* But this time, I had a plan. While sitting in jail, I decided to make a better life for me and my child. I realized that God will hide you in order to prepare you for greater. I was ready to come out of hiding. I trusted God to restore everything I had lost. I did not have a date of when it would happen, I just knew it would. And he did. Over and over again. I took that 19 day journey and created a transformation program for women. I now own 3 prosperous and profitable companies. I don't skip details any more. I make sure all documents are together. I am happily married and we have a beautiful daughter together as well. Fear convinced me to hide from my past. But it's my past that granted me the path to do the life changing work I do now. So, no fear, I'm not hiding. And you can't have it. My true freedom from fear has come from discovering who God has created me to be and what He has equipped me to do on purpose.

I opened by talking to fear; now, I want to talk to you.

What have you lost hope in because of fear?

_____

_____

_____

What change can you decide to make today to get your hope back?

_____

_____

_____

About the Author

Shalon Barnett is passionate about serving others and has spent a lifetime helping people in need. Her story is one of struggle, inner strength, and triumph. Shalon has owned several profitable businesses, including a group home for special needs individuals. As co-owner of North Tampa Pharmacy and a registered pharmacy technician, Shalon is also a member of the Florida Board of Pharmacy Association and the NAACP (National Association for the Advancement of Colored People). Shalon's mantra and mission statement of

HOPE is "Helping Other People Excel." Shalon established Shalon's HOPE, a non-profit organization, to empower women and help them overcome a history of abuse, bad relationships and criminal records. The organization allows Shalon to publicly do what she has done privately for years; give to individuals and organizations. As a speaker, Shalon shares her story of poverty, battery and shame to inspire others to change, discover their purpose and live their dreams. Shalon has received numerous awards and was featured recently in the online publication Glambitious Magazine for her work with Shalon's HOPE. Shalon has been married to the love of her life, Jamaal Barnett, for four years. They are the proud parents of four children.

IMPACT

BY TIANA PATRICE

dear fear, you can't have my ...

Dear fear,

You Can't Have My Impact

There's a story in the bible that I love. It's the story of Elijah and the Widow of Zarephath. In this story, God instructed Elijah to go to Zarephath where there would be a widow waiting for him to supply him with food. When Elijah got to the widow, she told him that she didn't have enough, as she was already preparing sticks to go home, cook her last meal, and die. Elijah told her to not be afraid, but to go home and prepare the meal as she had said, first bringing some to him, and then to herself and her son. He told her that God said, the flour would not be used up and the oil would not run dry. And it did not. I love this story because it's a direct reflection of God's love for us. You see it doesn't matter what we say, what matters is God's perfect will. Much like the widow of Zarephath, we tend to speak death over our lives, and quickly give up our faith for fear. We believe what fear or the enemy has told us about our situation, and turn our ears from what God has promised. But because he loves us so much, he will send help when we need it. He will always provide the provision for the vision, even when our faith doesn't match up. Just like God wasn't checking the widow's cabinets, he isn't checking your bank account, or likes on social media...he is checking for your faith and obedience.

In 2015 shortly after Fifty Two Shades of Fearless was launched, God gave me another vision. This time the vision was to launch a movement. Like the widow, I begin to speak death over my impact instead of immediately giving God my yes. I began to send his calls to voicemail, and when I did pick up I negotiated. You see I thought I had done everything he wanted me to do...but there was more. And there still is. I learned that Fifty Two Shades of Fearless was just the platform to set me up as the expert in my field. It was my new business card, and my way in to do what he was really calling me to do. "A movement", I said. "But I'm not that popular, I don't have a huge following, I don't have that many social media likes or shares. Who am I?" While I questioned who I was, God reminded me WHOSE I was.

In that season, I launched the movement, A Million Fearless Strong, where our mission is to liberate the lives of 1 Million women from fear. How do we do this? Through our online communities, speaking, training, books, coaching, consulting and The Fearless Tour which is an experience where we hit the road and take the message of living Fearless from city to city. When I launched this movement, I had less than $100 in my bank account, I still didn't have the likes or the following. But I had faith. Since then, this movement has reached thousands all over the world, I've been a guest contributor for FORBES, including being invited to the Forbes Coaches council for my work, I've launched more than 15 authors into the world, I've shared stages with greats, and graced over 30 stages sharing the message of Activate Your FearLESS, I received an award in New Delhi, India, and have been featured in The Huffington Post, ABC, CBS, NBC, plus more...Am I bragging? Come on you should know me better than that by now. I'm not sharing this for me, because it's not about me. This is so much bigger than me...I am just the vessel God is using today.

Fear tried to convince me that I wasn't enough, that I wasn't qualified. I was seeking validation in my bank account and social status. But God reminded me that he qualified me a long time ago for such a time as this. These are my receipts for activating my fearless. Every time you make the bold, courageous and conscious choice to fear less you open up a new level to your faith and purpose, you open up new opportunities to use your gifts and you please God. You enter into a season where you begin to SEE what God has said!

By making the decision to do life differently, to give God my unconditional yes and obedience, I've been able to access opportunities and kingdom connections available on the other side. So no fear, not today. You can't have my impact. You can't have my evidence. You can't have the lives that's being changed through God using me. You can't have it. I am on assignment, and until God says, "Well done my good and faithful servant", you fear are the one that should be afraid.

What impact could you be making on the world, if only you weren't afraid?

_____

_____

_____

What can you do TODAY to begin using your influence and power to make positive change?

_____

_____

_____

What's Next

Right now, you're in the middle of a shift. You know there is more for you, but you don't quite know how to get there. You know you are destined for greater but unsure what that looks like. You feel the urge to serve, but unsure in what capacity. I get exactly where you are. In 2014, I was being pulled between my fear and my purpose. I knew there was so much more I could be doing, but fear of rejection, success and failure kept me in places far longer that I should have been. However, in June of 2014 I realized that what God was asking me to let go of, was nothing compared to what he was getting ready to bless me with, and I made a life changing decision that would shift the entire trajectory of my life. I didn't know all of the answers, I didn't know all of the steps to take, but I learned that sometimes the only step you can take is out on faith. Are you ready to do something different? Are you ready to do something bold like taking that next step into greater and serving in your purpose? If so...then head over to www.yournextisnow.com to learn more about partnering with Women's CEO Alliance, to get the tools you need to live the life you have always imagined.

Your NEXT is waiting, on the other side of your fear….

are you ready?

www.yournextisnow.com

Special Thanks To

Jeremy Toliver of

Phase ONE Photography

For Photography & Videography Solutions
Contact Jeremy Toliver
334-479-3412
phase1photography@gmail.com

Special Thanks To
Tiphanny Andrews & Alexis Davis of
#BeatByTip

Contact Tiphanny Andrews for the ultimate
#BeatByTip Experience
www.beatbytip.com
makeupbytip@gmail.com
678-300-7300

FEARLESS

BY TY SCOTT KING

Dear Fear,

There was a time when I felt trapped by you
I accepted your lies and doubts
and carried them on my shoulders- like boulders-
from under which I could not get out.
I allowed your seed of inferiority to grow
then take authority- come to fruition
Opportunities came and passed
as I spent days and nights avoiding my mission.
Distressed about my destiny
Unable to see-
Lacking vision
Thoughts of a bleak future
My hope- arrested and imprisoned.

Then, one day I heard of The Fearless Movement
Where women dared to be courageous
And operate in their gifts and talents
Their superpowers were contagious.

So, Fear,
I'm letting you know now-
Your times up
I'm letting you go now
You no longer have control.
I'm reclaiming my passions
aligning my actions
I'm ready to be bold!
To subtract you from my equation
And add more hope, love, and faith
Abandon average. Walk in purpose.
Because I'm destined to be great!
I'm moving forward to live my best life
To rise like I'm weightless
I'm removing myself from the waitlist
Headed to the front of the line.

My time is here
My moment is now
I refuse to be left behind!
And I don't need anyone to cosign
because my way has been paved by The Divine

I am no longer powerless
I stride with confidence
One fearless step at a time!
©2017. Ty Scott King